CW01521810

Windows 11 for Seniors: 2021
Complete User Guide to Master
Your Microsoft Windows 11
Operating System

Copyright © 2022

All rights reserved.

ISBN: 9798781521821

© Copyright 2022 - All rights reserved.

The content contained within this book may not be reproduced, duplicated or transmitted without direct written permission from the author or the publisher.

Under no circumstances will any blame or legal responsibility be held against the publisher, or author, for any damages, reparation, or monetary loss due to the information contained within this book. Either directly or indirectly. You are responsible for your own choices, actions, and results.

Legal Notice:

This book is copyright protected. This book is only for personal use. You cannot amend, distribute, sell, use, quote or paraphrase any part, or the content within this book, without the consent of the author or publisher.

Disclaimer Notice:

Please note the information contained within this document is for educational and entertainment purposes only. All effort has been executed to present accurate, up to date, and reliable, complete information. No warranties of any kind are declared or implied. Readers acknowledge that the author is not engaging in the rendering of legal, financial, medical or professional advice. The content within this book has been derived from various sources. Please consult a licensed professional before attempting any techniques outlined in this book.

By reading this document, the reader agrees that under no circumstances is the author responsible for any losses, direct or indirect, which are incurred as a result of the use of the information contained within this document, including, but not limited to, — errors, omissions, or inaccuracies.

CONTENTS:

Introduction

What is Windows 11?

Microsoft began sending out Windows 11 as a free update to the majority of Windows 10 users on Oct. 5. If you are running Windows 8, you must first upgrade to Windows 10 for free, and then download Windows 11. Before you decide whether or not to install the new operating system, let's discuss what we like and dislike about it.

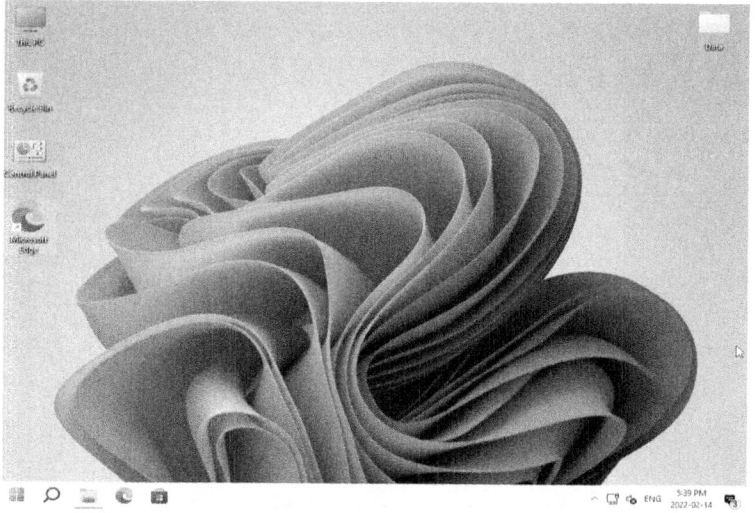

A user-friendly operating system, whether it's MacOS on your MacBook or Google's Wear OS on your smartwatch, improves with increased transparency. And that user is you when you type on a laptop keyboard or tap on a smartphone screen. Regrettably, there are no Spinal Tap "goes to 11" puns here. That is primarily due to the fact that Windows 11 seems more like Windows 10.5 than a generational leap – not that there is anything fundamentally wrong with that.

Perhaps the transition from Windows 10 to Windows 11 feels minor in comparison to the leap from Windows 8 to Windows 10. Microsoft even skipped an entire version number due to its size. That generation was focused on righting a ship that had veered too far into tablet territory, convincing everyone that Windows laptops and tablets were just as cool as iPads. They are not, and that is fine: I work on a Windows system and do a lot of PC gaming on it, but I use an iPad to read news headlines in bed at night.

Windows 10 began with favorable reviews and has maintained that position exactly because it stayed out of the way of whatever you were doing rather than attempting to impose its beliefs on you. However, it was free* — with an asterisk to signify that it was widely available for free to anyone with a non-ancient PC.

Who is eligible to receive Windows 11?

To be honest, the list of compatible PCs is a little shorter than I anticipated. A 64-bit processor, 4GB of RAM, 64GB of storage, UEFI secure boot, and TPM (trusted platform module) 2.0 are required as minimum requirements. That last one can be problematic for some users, particularly on less expensive laptops. If your CPU is older than the seventh-generation Intel Core series (we're currently up to the 11th-generation), you may be in trouble. To do a check, download and run the Microsoft PC Health Check app. There are solutions available for installing Windows 11, but use them at your own peril.

Visual indicators

If there is one element about Windows 11 that quickly stands out, it is this: Instead of being positioned to the left by default, the start menu and taskbar are now centered on the bottom of the screen. Yes, that is the single most significant aesthetic and interface change that will occur on day one. While there is certainly more going on beyond the surface, it appears as though this UI transition is primarily intended to alert you to the fact that something new and different is occurring beneath the surface.

Additionally, Windows 11 has a lot going on. You're unlikely to notice much of it if you're a casual or mainstream user, but there are a few noteworthy upgrades worth noting.

One of the primary selling points of Chromebooks, which run Google's ChromeOS operating system, is that the majority of Chromebooks can run virtually any Android app, from phone-centric favorites like Instagram to mobile games. This liberates Chromebooks from their reliance on cloud-based applications and, frankly, adds a lot of functionality to your $300 Chromebook.

Microsoft is incorporating comparable capability into Windows 11 in order to compete with Chromebooks and to strengthen ties between Windows PC and Android phone users, just how Macs and iPhones are inextricably linked.

That's unfortunate because easy access to Android apps was perhaps the most significant practical change in Windows 11 for the majority of users. While there are alternative methods, such as utilizing an app like Bluestacks or even Microsoft's Your Phone, they are not simple enough for ordinary users.

Multiple desktops and snap groups

Once you get the hang of it, grouping a collection of open windows so you can see and access them when you want – and hide them when you don't – is quite useful. While the option to snap windows into preset slots on the desktop has been for some time, the new Snap Groups and Snap Layouts provide some more methods to organize your windows.

By hovering your cursor over the "maximize" button in the top right corner of most windows, a pop-up window displaying a variety of layout options will appear. When you minimize these apps, you may restore them to their original locations by hovering over any of the snapped window icons in the taskbar.

However, not every application I tried permitted me to snap its window. While web browsers, system utilities, and a variety of other unrelated apps did, Photoshop and Steam did not (hovering over their maximize buttons did not bring up the snapping choices pop-up menu).

It's useful if you have a massive monitor, use numerous monitors, or need to open several thinly sliced web browser windows simultaneously. On a laptop screen, you're usually just viewing one or sometimes two windows at a time.

Multiple desktops are a typical macOS feature and a convenient way to arrange various aspects of your digital life. For instance, you can maintain all of your professional applications on one desktop — email programs, browsers, and video conferencing applications — and all of your gaming applications on another. As with a Mac, you can hot-swap between them; the only difference is in the way your open programs are presented.

You can do the same thing in Windows 10, but it's a nuisance. In Windows 11, desktops come pre-configured with their own taskbar icon, and establishing and arranging numerous desktops is even easier than on a Mac, which is not something you hear very frequently.

They've returned. On the plus side, each of the new widgets has its own taskbar button, making them easy to locate. When the button is pressed, a semi-transparent panel appears from the screen's left edge.

By default, it includes widgets for the weather, your Outlook calendar, any images stored in OneDrive, and a To-Do list. You can customize the list somewhat, although there are not a lot of possibilities at the moment. Below that is a newsfeed that appears to have been curated by the same folks that curate the news on the Microsoft Edge browser's home screen. You may conceal stories from any outlet by clicking on a menu icon in the news section or by clicking on a "manage your interests" button to modify the feed, although it's quite basic by default. Numerous sports, Fox News, and celebrity gossip segments.

Additional enhancements to one's quality of life

I take a lot of screen images since I frequently refer to system tools, settings menus, and other on-screen items in my work. That's simple on a Mac — Shift + Command + 4. In Windows, though, it has never been quite that straightforward. The built-in Snipping tool, on the other hand, is slightly less obnoxious with Windows 11. Now you can capture a screenshot by pressing Windows + Shift + S; while this copies the screenshot to the clipboard, it does not save the image automatically; you must still do so manually.

The Edge browser now includes a secure Kids Mode, which is accessible by clicking on your profile in the top right corner and can be configured for various age groups.

Auto HDR – a function carried over from the Xbox Series X – boosts lighting, brightness, and contrast in games that do not support high dynamic range for a more HDR-like image.

I'm anticipating a redesigned Microsoft app store that will include third-party services such as gaming stores and web browsers. The Opera browser is currently available; the Epic Games storefront is slated to launch shortly. There is yet no word on alternative browsers such as Firefox or Chrome, or on the popular Steam PC gaming marketplace. Android app support will eventually be provided by an Amazon-branded Android app store rather than Google Play.

Who is the best candidate for Windows 11?

Despite my ambivalent attitude on the new Windows operating system, there are no compelling reasons to avoid it. That is because any new PC operating system begins incomplete, with the biggest enhancements and most polished versions arriving later, from Windows 8.1 to Windows 10 Creators Edition.

I've been using various preview builds of Windows 11 on multiple PCs for months, alongside the final release build, and everything has been fine, nearly completely trouble-free, and I've never considered switching back to Windows 10.

Having said that, Microsoft will occasionally be Microsoft. Certain long-standing Windows annoyances have persisted. When setting up the OS for the first time, there are still a plethora of options for data sharing and ad personalization to uncheck, and the built-in Edge browser buries the default search engine settings (to switch from Bing too, say, Google) several submenus deep. Changing which apps do what by default is also more complicated today; you literally have to assign each file type —.htm,.html, and so on — individually.

Hopefully, this will become more streamlined in the future.

If you purchase a new laptop or desktop computer after today, it will almost certainly come pre-installed with Windows 11. In that situation, there is no need to make a conscious choice; simply go with the flow. If you own a current-generation Windows laptop, tablet, or desktop computer, you can download and install Windows 11 now or in the near future.

As a general rule, I recommend that you avoid becoming the first person on the block to download a new operating system update, regardless of whether it's for your laptop, phone, or tablet. Issues will surely arise, if only due to the enormous variety of hardware configurations and peripherals, from printers to mice to virtual reality headsets, that must function properly.

Having said that, testing for Windows 11 has been thorough, and the primary concerns thus far have been with the way icons are displayed, some menu inconsistencies, and the occasional File Explorer crash.

How to install a new OS?

Everyone using Windows 10 is eligible for a free upgrade if they have a suitable PC, but many people are still waiting.

Because Microsoft is releasing the OS in stages, your system may not ask you to upgrade immediately – in fact, you may not even notice it if you set your computer to check for updates. Microsoft stated in an August blog post that "all eligible devices will be offered a free upgrade to Windows 11 by mid-2022." Want to avoid waiting till next year? Continue reading to learn how the Windows 11 Installation Assistant can serve as a shortcut to Windows 11.

If you're not in a hurry, the Windows 11 update will be pushed to your device in the following months when Microsoft determines the device is ready for the upgrade. When the new operating system becomes available, the upgrading process will be comparable to that of a standard Windows 10 update, as long as your device is compatible and matches the required minimum requirements. (And even if it does not, Microsoft will provide a fix, but your Windows 11 installation will no longer be supported.)

However, you may manually download Windows 11 and experiment with its new features, like widgets, snap layouts, virtual desktops, and the new Microsoft Store. We'll explain how to do so below. Before you begin your download, here is all the information you need to know about Microsoft's new software.

You may check to see if your current Windows 10 PC qualifies for the free upgrade to Windows 11 in a few different ways. Additionally, if you purchase a new computer, that computer will be eligible for the free update.

If you haven't updated to Windows 10 yet, don't despair - there is still a working way for obtaining Windows 10 for free. Now is an excellent time to make the transition so that your computer is prepared for the Windows 11 upgrade. That method is identical to the one used to manually upgrade an older machine to Windows 11, however, Microsoft does not recommend doing so because the machine may not be eligible for the same upgrades.

How to download Windows 11 without waiting

Certain customers can download Windows 11 in the same manner as they would any other new version of Windows. To check for updates, navigate to Settings > Update & Security > Windows Update and click the Check for Updates button. If accessible, you'll notice the Windows 11 feature update. To download and install, click.

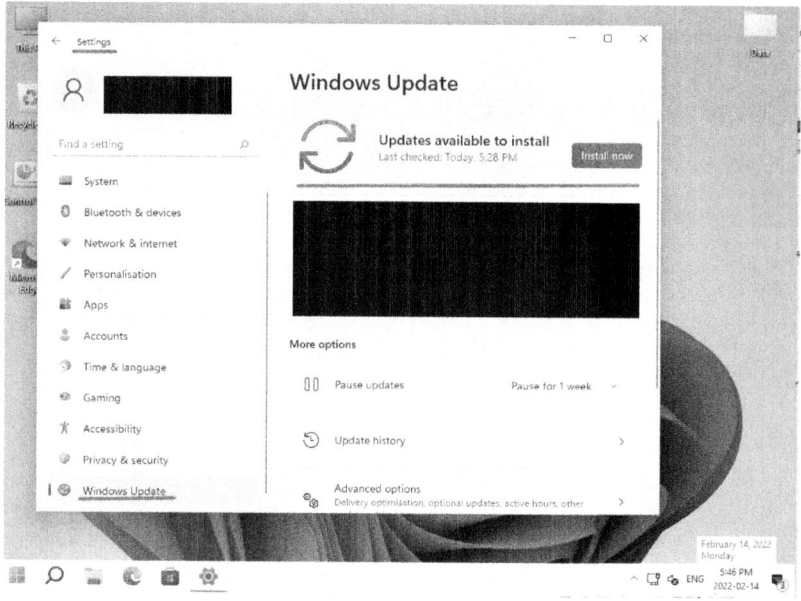

Again, keep in mind that the Windows 11 rollout will be gradual — it could be months before your device receives the update. The upgrade will begin with new PCs and will roll out to all compatible devices by mid-2022, depending on the device's age and hardware.

If you do not currently have access to the upgrade but wish to do so, you have a few options. The quickest and most straightforward method is to download the Windows 11 Installation Assistant. After downloading, select Run to verify that your hardware is compatible. Then click Accept and Install to confirm your agreement with the license terms and to begin the installation. When the installation is complete, you will be required to restart your computer. Do not be frightened if your computer restarts numerous times during the installation procedure. Simply leave your computer on till everything is completed.

If you are unable to use the Windows 11 Installation Assistant, you have a few backup choices, but they are more involved. We strongly suggest you consider waiting for your device to receive the update. If you are convinced to want to proceed, you can produce installation media for Windows 11 or an ISO file. Microsoft's download Windows 11 page goes into additional detail about those methods.

What is included in Windows 11?

Windows 11 introduces a new streamlined style with pastel colors, softer corners, a new startup sound, and a more Mac-like overall appearance. The Windows Start menu has been relocated to the center of the screen, with app icons grouped in the center alongside it. You'll discover a slew of new desktop utilities, like widgets that provide quick access to information and a simplified virtual desktop setup. Additionally, Android applications will be integrated into Windows and accessible via the Microsoft Store – albeit this functionality will not be available immediately.

The upgrade is the first significant modification to Microsoft's operating system since the debut of Windows 10 in 2015. For the last year, rumors about a significant Windows redesign have circulated. On May 25, CEO Satya Nadella announced that Microsoft was planning "one of the most substantial updates to Windows in the last decade," confirming that a huge shift was on the horizon for the OS's 1.3 billion users in 2021. And in mid-June, Microsoft secretly revealed that it would discontinue support for Windows 10 in 2025 in response to the emergence of leaked photos of Windows 11.

Chapter 1: Microsoft features

Microsoft Edge

Microsoft rebuilt Edge from the ground up using the open-source Chromium project's core, which is also used by Google Chrome. Existing Chrome users will immediately recognize the new Edge, which is by design. At first glance, the new Edge appears to be nothing more than Chrome with a Microsoft logo slapped across the front.

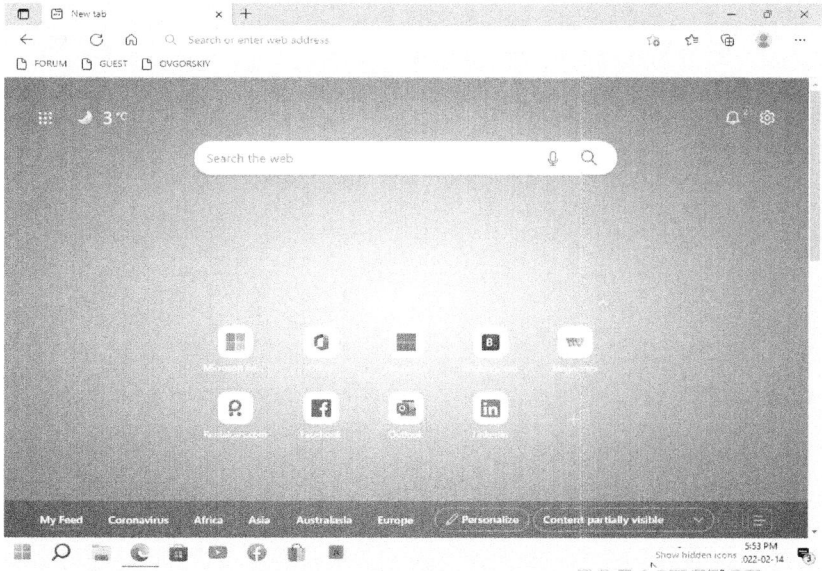

However, if one digs a bit deeper, one discovers that there is much more going on here. I believe there is a true market for a Chrome browser that does not communicate with Google's servers, and Microsoft's new Edge browser fills that void. It integrates with your

Microsoft Account and has fully customizable tracking prevention options. With the new Edge, Microsoft is prioritizing privacy. Additionally, it is enterprise-ready, with support for AAD and an Internet Explorer mode for rendering legacy websites, among other features.

While this is all well and good, we're interested in learning whether the new Microsoft Edge is a good browser for users outside of the enterprise. Should you, as a typical PC user, upgrade to the new Microsoft Edge browser? There is a lot here that standard PC users will like, such as cross-platform syncing if you also use Microsoft Edge on macOS, iOS, or Android. Additionally, it is the only browser on Windows 10 that supports Netflix 4K streaming.

Since the new Microsoft Edge entered preview in the spring of last year, and the release candidate in November, I've been using it. Now that the new Microsoft Edge is available, I wanted to write a review for anyone considering switching from another browser. Whether you're a long-time user of Microsoft Edge or a die-hard Google Chrome supporter, I believe that everyone should pay attention to Microsoft's new browser.

The Positive

- Outstanding web performance
- A Familiar User Interface
- Access to extensions built on the Chromium platform
- Google Chrome sans Google

The Negative

- At launch, there is no history synchronization.
- Several functions, such as inking into web pages, are missing.
- Install Microsoft Edge

Configuration of Microsoft Edge

Let us begin from the beginning. If you were previously using Microsoft Edge, installing and upgrading to the new browser is a breeze. Whether you install the browser manually or wait for Microsoft to do so via Windows Update, the new browser will replace the old one and import all of your data. In a matter of seconds, the first run wizard will migrate everything of your passwords, history, bookmarks, and more to the new Edge.

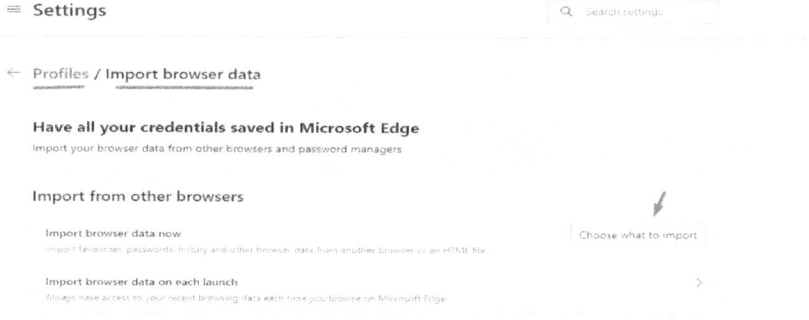

Those migrating from a third-party browser will need to navigate to the new Edge's settings page to integrate their data, but everything should import without trouble. Microsoft is making the procedure as simple as possible, knowing full well that the onerous effort of switching browsers is a deal-breaker for many. After installing the updated Edge, you should be up and running in less than a minute with all your data intact.

One feature that has not been carried over from the previous Microsoft Edge is extensions. When users migrate to the new Edge, they will need to manually download all their extensions anew. Fortunately, the new Microsoft Edge supports the same extensions as Google Chrome, which means you won't be without your beloved extensions.

While your Microsoft Account is used to sync browser data across devices, history and open tabs are not yet synced. This implies that if you attempt to switch to the new Edge on numerous devices, you will be unable to view cross-device history or open tabs on additional devices.

This also means that the new Microsoft Edge does not support the Timeline feature included in Windows 10. Microsoft does state that these additional sync settings will ultimately become visible, but no date has been specified. Personally, I'm not concerned, but I understand that the inability to sync history across devices may be a deal-breaker for some. If that is the case, I recommend that you wait for all sync settings to become available before giving the new Edge a try. Microsoft is currently working on it.

Microsoft Edge Internet Explorer browsing experience

Once everything is configured, the first thing you'll notice is the new tab page, which has been brought over from the previous version of Microsoft Edge and enhanced with additional personalization options. By default, the browser uses Bing to search the web, although users can modify this setting in the browser's settings. The new tab page will automatically list your most frequently visited websites and will also allow you to manually pin websites.

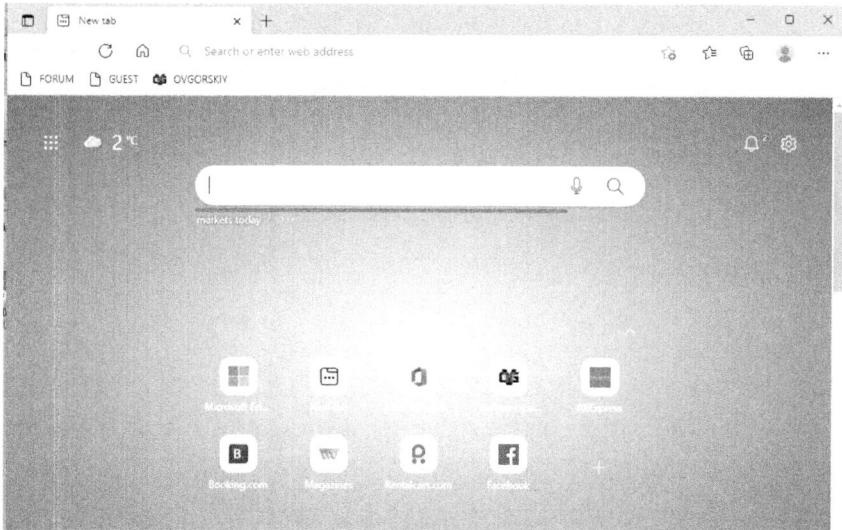

Below that, you may opt for MSN to display a grid of recent news articles, and you can even tailor which topics appear here. I'm aware that some users dislike being inundated with information on their new tab page, which is why this is completely customizable. If you don't want to see any news stories, you can completely disable them.

Additionally, you can toggle on or off a daily wallpaper that is pulled in from Bing, which adds a little flair to your new tab page. This is something I leave off because I want a more simple aesthetic. However, if you enjoy watching the news or seeing a fresh image each day, those are configuration possibilities.

The UI along the top of the browser is intentionally similar to that of Google Chrome. Microsoft aims to make the transition from previous browsers to the new Microsoft Edge as pleasant as possible, which includes making the new Edge look identical to other browsers. If you're a Google Chrome user switching to the new Microsoft Edge, you'll find all of your imported data in the same places it was in Chrome.

This lowers the entry hurdle. Users dislike change, and by making the new Edge nearly identical to Google Chrome, Chrome users will feel less overwhelmed when moving to the new Edge. Having said that, there are a few modest changes to the user interface that bring the browser more in line with Microsoft's own design language. The corners are a little more angular, and the settings area is quite different as well.

Browsing the web is a breeze. The days of the previous Edge being incompatible or rendering web pages poorly are over. The new Microsoft Edge browser is fast, fluid, and intuitive to use. Indeed, the web browsing experience is now similar to Chrome, as Microsoft Edge is built on the same open-source Chromium project as Google Chrome.

I have not had the new Microsoft Edge crashing on me, nor have I noticed it struggling to render web pages such as YouTube. The previous Microsoft Edge was infamous for its inability to render Google-centric websites, while the new Microsoft Edge simply does not have that issue. Users of the previous version of Edge will also appreciate the ability to conceal the buttons featured along the browser's top bar. You can conceal the favorites button if you don't want it up there.

Web applications for Microsoft Edge

The option to install webpages as native apps is a new capability for Edge users. This functionality is advantageous if you utilize a service that does not have a specific PC application. Gmail is an outstanding illustration of this. Google has not created a specific Gmail app for Windows 10, but with the new Microsoft Edge, you can simply install the Gmail website as an app and it will appear in the Start menu and run in its own window exactly like a genuine app.

If you're coming from Google Chrome, this is not a new feature, but Microsoft has worked to make these online apps appear more native to Windows. While this feature is not available yet, a future update will make web apps seem to Windows as if they were native applications. This means they'll appear as their own task in Task Manager, and notifications will appear in the Action Center under the website's specific name.

When Windows 10X is released next year, this functionality will become even more critical. For the time being, it serves as an excellent method of pinning your favorite websites to your taskbar and Startmenu.

Microsoft Edge anti-tracking

One notable feature Microsoft is emphasizing as part of the new Microsoft Edge is its own tracking prevention capabilities. Privacy is a hot topic these days, and Microsoft is well aware of this. To assist users in their pursuit of greater privacy, the new Microsoft Edge has an easy-to-use tracking protection feature that is enabled by default.

Microsoft offers three levels of tracking prevention, with the default setting being Balanced. This option automatically blocks trackers from websites you haven't visited and also blocks known malicious trackers. This option is intended to make your data as private as possible while without interfering with the operation of websites. Level one allows the majority of websites to track you, whereas level three allows almost no websites to track you unless you explicitly grant permission.

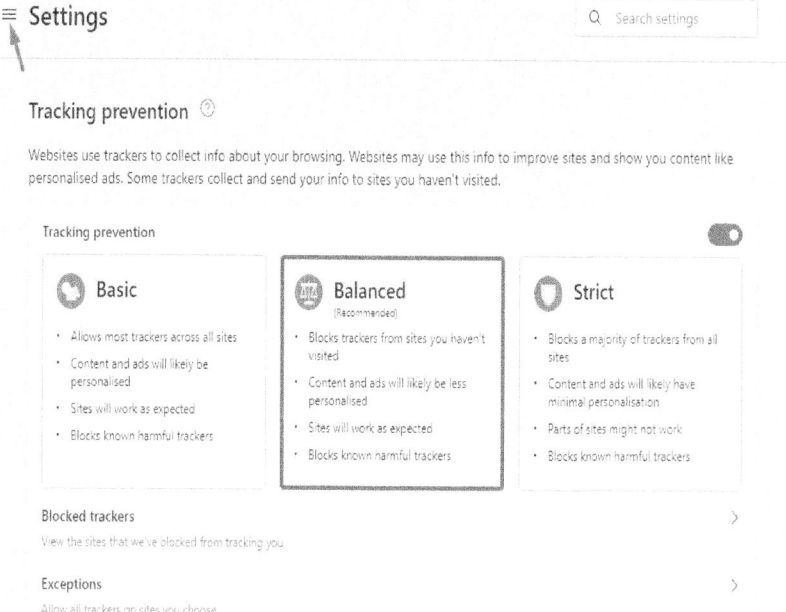

It's fantastic to see this level of tracking prevention included directly into the new Microsoft Edge, and it's also fully adjustable. Users can add their own websites to a forbidden or exceptions list to control whether or not a certain website tracks or does not track them. Additionally, there is a straightforward UI for clearing browsing data, as well as the option to delete certain data each time the browser is closed. If you're concerned about your privacy, the new Edge browser goes to considerable measures to ensure that you feel secure while using it. While it is not the most privacy-conscious browser available, it is an excellent first step for Microsoft.

Collections for Microsoft Edge

The collection is a spiritual successor to the previous Microsoft Edge's "put tabs aside" feature. Collections let you organize links, photos, and snippets into a reference list for further reference. This is extremely beneficial for students conducting a study on a particular subject, or for chefs looking for inspiration for their next creation, for example.

The Collections feature is accessible from any webpage and is located at the top of the URL bar. Although I haven't found much use for it yet, I can see how this feature fits with Microsoft's ethos of "be more productive." You may also simply import your collections to Excel and Word if desired.

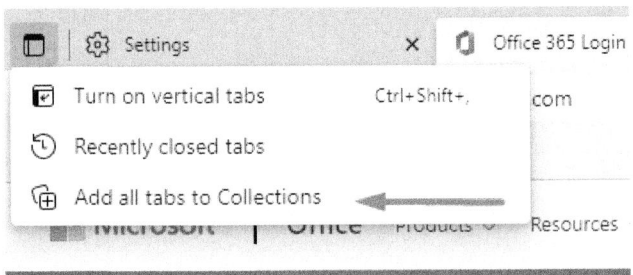

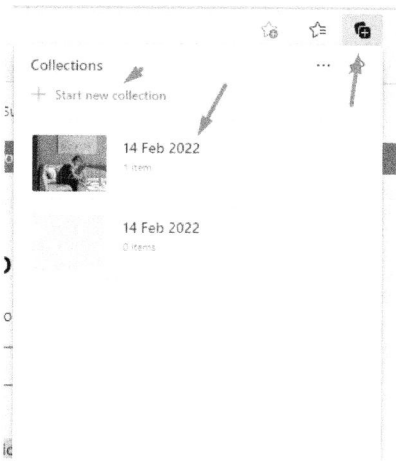

Additionally, it syncs to the cloud, allowing you to access your stored collections across all of your Microsoft Edge-enabled devices, including mobile.

What is missing from Microsoft Edge?

While there is a lot new in the new Microsoft Edge, there is also a lot that is missing from the previous Microsoft Edge. Tab management, linking into web pages, Fluent Design, and Timeline support are all absent from the new Microsoft Edge. Microsoft says it is evaluating which improvements to add to the latest version of Microsoft Edge, with enhanced inking capabilities being one of them. However, not every feature is assured to make the cut, which is a crying shame.

Additionally, several testers believe that the older Microsoft Edge is superior at handling touch and scrolling. Personally, I don't perceive any difference between the two browsers, although die-hard Microsoft Edge supporters argue that the new browser is poorer at scrolling and touch interaction than the old one. The new Edge is not incompetent in any of these areas; it just implies that the previous Microsoft Edge was great in these areas.

Microsoft's new Edge browser is fantastic. It represents a significant shift from the previous Microsoft Edge, which struggled in a number of areas. If you previously attempted to move to the older Microsoft Edge, I strongly advise you to give the new Microsoft Edge a try. It's a whole new ballgame that functions and performs significantly better.

Some die-hard fans of the previous Microsoft Edge may object to the absence of elements that made the old Edge special, but those users are already in the minority. This browser's primary goal is to be accessible to the widest possible audience, which it accomplishes admirably. There are no strange elements that obstruct your browsing experience.

Microsoft's decision to use Chromium for Edge is the finest it has made in a long time for a failing product. Rather than abandoning Edge totally, Microsoft chose to restart, and the result is a product that I believe can truly compete in the browser sector. I'd even venture to suggest that many Chrome users won't mind moving to the new Edge, and may even prefer it to Chrome.

Microsoft Edge tips

1. User interface

Microsoft Edge's user interface has been totally overhauled, but the familiar look and feel of the older version have been retained to decrease the learning curve.

The new interface is simple, modern, and elegant, with rounded edges that make the browser more welcoming, and because it is built on the Chromium open-source platform, the visual elements are comparable to those found in the Chrome browser. However, this is not a negative thing, as the majority of modern browsers appear the same in any case.

When you initially launch the browser, you'll find a similar layout to the previous version, with tabs in the top-left corner, navigation controls on the left, the address bar in the center, and action buttons on the right.

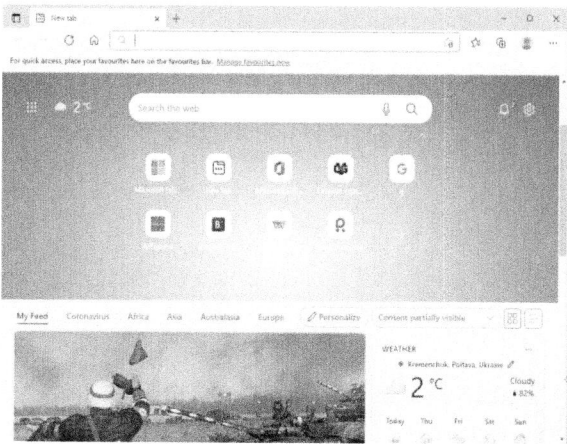

The "Settings and more" menu appears to be identical to the legacy version, however many of the options have been updated.

Perhaps the most significant interface enhancement is the new settings experience, which has evolved from a flyout menu to a full-page structure, making options easier to find and adjust.

2. Profiles

One of the nicest features in the Chromium-based version of Microsoft Edge is "Profiles," which, as the name implies, allows you to establish profiles (accounts) to share the browser with other people without creating additional accounts on Windows 10.

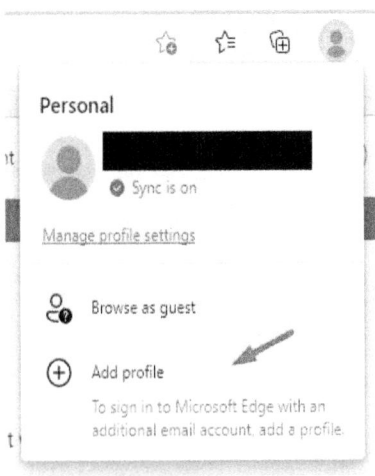

Additionally, because profiles segregate data (favorites, passwords, payment information, addresses, history, extensions, and other settings), you can use them to establish different profiles for yourself to separate personal and professional staff.

By default, the browser creates a profile for you, but you can always edit, add, or remove profiles using the browser settings.

Microsoft Edge recognizes two distinct sorts of profiles. You can build a local profile that is not linked to the internet; this profile's settings will be available only on the device. Alternatively, you can connect your Microsoft account to create a cloud profile, which will allow you to backup your settings and sync data between devices.

3. Preventative surveillance

Along with the new rendering engine, Microsoft Edge introduces a new privacy feature called "Tracking prevention" that protects you from online tracking.

While you visit a website, online trackers can collect information about your internet activity (such as visited sites, clicks, and interests) using cookies and a variety of other technologies (even when you are not active on the page). And then businesses use this information to target you with adverts and provide a more personalized experience.

Tracking prevention is enabled by default, and it contains a range of settings for configuring how the browser detects and blocks malicious web trackers from gathering your activity in order to protect your privacy.

This option is accessible via the "Privacy and services" settings.

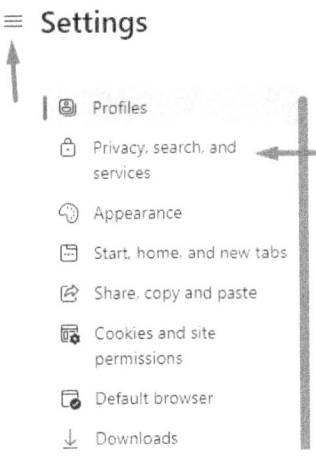

While "Balanced" is the recommended level, you can also choose "Basic," which blocks malicious trackers but permits some tracking. Alternatively, you can select the "Strict" option, which disables almost all trackers but is likely to damage the majority of websites and visual components on the page.

4. Chrome add-ons

As a result of the migration to an open-source platform, Microsoft Edge is now compatible with a number of capabilities previously available only to Google Chrome users, including extensions.

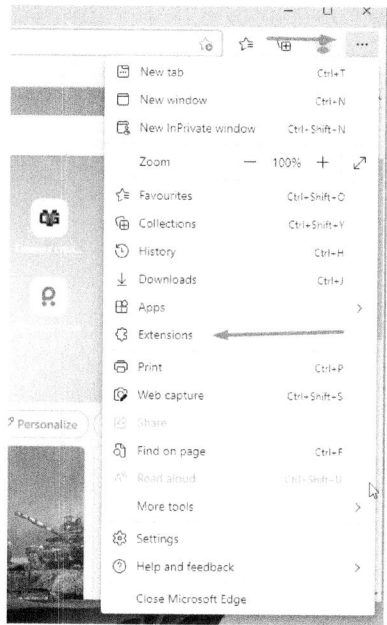

If you're new with extensions (or addons), they're small programs that you may put on a web browser to enhance its usefulness, increase its security, or modify its behavior. Typically, an extension performs a single function.

Although the new Microsoft Edge has its own extension shop, you can also install Chrome extensions via the Chrome Web Store. All you need to do is select the "Extensions" settings option to install extensions from other stores.

5. Web Apps That Are Progressive (PWAs)

Support for Progressive Web Apps is another excellent feature included with the new Microsoft Edge.

Progressive Web Apps is a Windows 10 technology that enables the installation and operation of webpages as native programs.

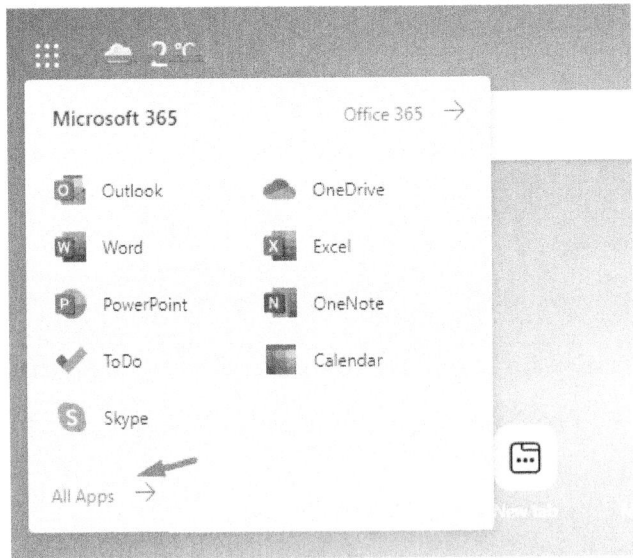

The ability to work offline, push notifications, rapid installs, instant loading and automated server-side updates are just a few of the unique features of web apps. Additionally, to create a more app-like experience, websites installed via the Chromium version of Edge will appear in the Start menu's "All apps" section, which can be easily removed via the "Apps & features settings" page. Although nearly any website can be installed as a Progressive Web App, developers are responsible for implementing the offered functionality.

6. Reader Immersive

When you're attempting to read a fascinating article online, it can be difficult to focus on the content due to the graphic components, advertisements, and links around it. Immersive Reader (formerly known as "Reading view") is a Microsoft Edge feature that eliminates distractions with a single click, allowing you to focus on the primary material.

Once you click the "Immersive Reader" button on the right side of the URL bar, the feature will remove all the clutter and re-format the content with more readable font and a warm-colored background.

Additionally, you may click the "Read aloud" button to have the voice engine read the text aloud at various rates and in a variety of voices.

7. Adobe Acrobat Reader

While most modern web browsers include the ability to work with PDF files, Microsoft Edge takes a somewhat different approach. Additionally, while opening PDF documents from the web or locally stored on your computer, you can choose some text and right-click to reveal the option to highlight the material; you can then save or print the document with the highlighted content.

Additionally, the PDF viewer supports inking. This means that you may now use the toolbar's Draw button to jot down notes and sketches. Additionally, this functionality is great for signing PDF documents without requiring third-party software installation. As with the highlighting function, you can save or print PDFs that have been inked. If you ever need to open a PDF document stored locally on your device, right-click it and then select the Open with menu, then Microsoft Edge.

8. Dark color scheme

If you like a dark color scheme, Microsoft Edge Chromium has you covered. As with the legacy version of the browser, the new version's "Appearance" options feature a dark theme option.

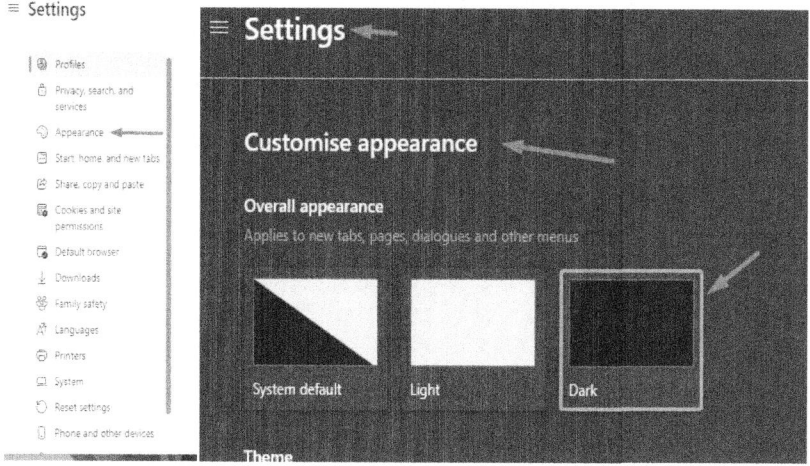

While on the settings page, you may toggle between bright and dark modes or select the "System default" option, which instructs Edge to swap theme colors when you alter the Windows 10 color scheme via the Settings app.

9. Collections

Additionally, Collection is a new feature in Microsoft Edge Chromium that enables you to easily collect photos, text, videos, and anything else you can drag and drop from the web into a collection group.

Although the feature is currently in development, if it is enabled in your installation, you will find it in the main menu. Once the feature is launched, all that is required is to click the Start new collection option. After giving the group a name, you can begin contributing links, photographs, and videos.

Additionally, you may click the button in the top-right corner to make notes, and you can export the content to an Excel or Word document via the collection context menu (three-dotted button).

You may use Collections for anything, but they're typically handier when you're shopping online and need to gather and compare product information prior to making a purchase. If you use the web browser for business or school, the feature can also be useful for conducting research, brainstorming ideas, creating lesson plans, and organizing excursions, among other things.

10. A more enjoyable browsing experience

While Microsoft has made significant efforts to give Microsoft Edge the greatest browser experience possible for Windows 10 customers, it has never been as fast or as compatible as Google Chrome. However, with Microsoft rebuilding Edge from the ground up using Google's Chromium engine, the browser is now faster than ever.

Additionally, having a more widely used open-source platform results in improved website and extension compatibility and less fragmentation, since developers no longer need to spend time and resources adapting their services to function on a separate platform. If a website or plugin is compatible with Google Chrome, it should also be compatible with Microsoft Edge.

Additionally, because Microsoft Edge is no longer tied to the Windows 10 development cycle, the company can now push new changes and features more quickly, and the browser is now cross-platform (Windows 10, macOS, iOS, Android, and Linux), significantly improving the browsing experience for everyone, regardless of the device they use.

Microsoft Office 365

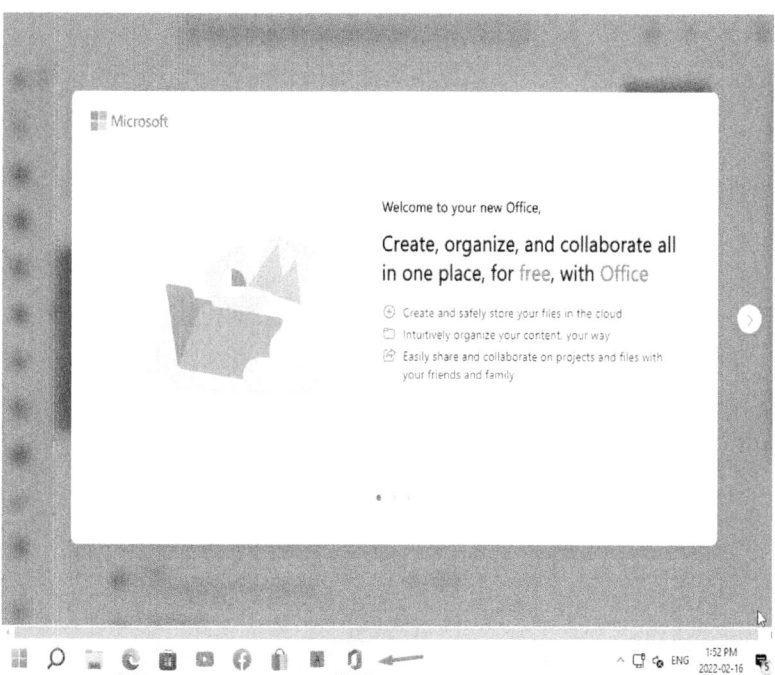

Microsoft 365—the new moniker for the programs and services that were previously known as Office 365—is the colossus of office suites,

the one that every competition attempts to emulate. It is available on practically every platform, including full-featured editions for Windows and macOS, surprisingly capable iOS and Android apps, and elegant web-based versions. Microsoft 365 includes all of the collaborative features seen in cloud-only suites such as Google Workspace, as well as the performance, security, and offline capabilities associated with disk-based apps. Microsoft's apps aren't ideal, and a few functions are cumbersome and unwieldy, but you'd have to have compelling reasons to use anything else. Microsoft 365 is a document-editing suite that has earned Editors' Choice status.

What Is the Price of Microsoft 365?

Microsoft 365 Personal subscriptions begin at $69.99 a year and include access to Microsoft Word, Excel, PowerPoint, OneNote, Outlook, and Skype apps for one user on up to five devices. Additionally, you receive Sway, which allows you to create interactive reports and presentations, forms for producing surveys and quizzes, and Microsoft's To-Do app. The $99.99-per-year Microsoft 365 Family tier, on the other hand, provides access to the same apps and supports up to six people. Additionally, this subscription tier includes the premium edition of the Microsoft Family app.

These prices are close to those offered by Google Workspace, which charges $6 and $12 per month for its Business Starter and Business Standard subscriptions, respectively. Microsoft's rates are significantly more than those of SoftMaker Office, which ranges from $29.90 to $49.90 per year, but SoftMaker lacks web-based products and offers just a beta version of an Android app.

Each subscription includes one terabyte of OneDrive storage for each user. Additionally, Microsoft allows two-factor authentication for web access, which is a welcome security feature.

For a one-time fee of $149.99, you can purchase a standalone version of Office Home & Student 2019 (traditional versions of Word, Excel, PowerPoint, and OneNote). This edition does not have automatic updates or OneDrive storage.

Microsoft 365 Business plans start at $5 per user per month and go up to $20 per user per month for the Business Premium plan. All Business subscriptions include cloud services for Teams, SharePoint, and Microsoft Exchange in addition to the Personal options. Windows-exclusive applications Publisher, which is used to create layouts that are too complex for Word, and Access, which is used to create databases, are both included in the Business packages. Business Premium subscribers receive tools for managing mobile devices and access to the Azure Information Protection service.

Microsoft 365 is available online or by download for Windows, macOS, Android, and iOS devices. Microsoft updated its macOS version lately with a new build that runs natively on Apple Silicon Macs (such as the current MacBook Air); these new programs perform astonishingly well.

The optimal office suite for you may very well be determined by the platforms and devices on which you work. Microsoft does not currently offer Office applications on Linux platforms—hopefully, the release of Edge for Linux signals that Microsoft will expand its support for those platforms. There is nothing preventing you from using any office suite's web-based version on Linux. LibreOffice and SoftMaker Office both offer specific applications for that platform.

Google Workspace is Microsoft 365's closest competitor, however, its apps are only available online. Except for a third-party version named Collabora Office, LibreOffice does not offer mobile apps. Softmaker Office and Corel WordPerfect Office are only available as desktop applications.

Numerous Features in Sleek Applications

The suite's basic applications—Word, Excel, PowerPoint, and Outlook—have evolved and changed for nearly forty years, and they're crammed with capabilities that can make them appear cumbersome and unwieldy in comparison to relative newbies like Apple's Pages and Numbers. Additionally, Microsoft continues to utilize a single software, Outlook, to manage email, contacts, calendars, and to-do lists, but other manufacturers, such as Apple and Google, have divided these functions into smaller, more streamlined apps that integrate seamlessly.

As with the majority of current word processors, Word provides overly complicated templates for organizing your own papers, but you're usually better off utilizing them as samples to learn from when creating your own.

Microsoft has obviously excelled itself in terms of the design of its separate office apps. They're aesthetically pleasing, extremely customizable, and feature a large UI that feels at ease on current technology in ways that competing apps do not. Microsoft is always upgrading its support for Dark Mode, and the latest additions include subtle color-shifting effects. These are currently accessible in the beta channel and will very certainly make their way into the release version shortly. Another neat technique is that if you alter a setting on one platform like the default color scheme, the change is automatically reflected in all of your Microsoft apps on other platforms. Although the ribbon can still be confusing—I have to constantly remind myself to go to the Insert tab to change an existing header or footer—a "Tell me what you want to accomplish" icon on the top-line menu allows me to quickly access the feature I'm looking for.

A Familiar Office Suite Continues to Improve

Word and Excel are among the most frequently used applications in the suite, and with good reason. Both run well, are impeccably polished, and receive frequent upgrades that improve their use. For example, while Excel already towers over other competing spreadsheet applications and is capable of handling massive worksheets without difficulty, Microsoft continues to add functionality. The LET function is a recent innovation that lets you to use named variables within a formula and repeat the function several times within a worksheet; this speeds up and simplifies calculations. This is a common occurrence with the types of upgrades that Microsoft 365 users receive but are not included in the standalone Office version.

Additionally, both Word and Excel have conveniences that no competition provides. For example, Word enables users to create lengthy documents while reading them in a mode that displays the page's real layout but hides the white space at the top and bottom of each printed page. This eliminates the need for two inches of white space between the beginning and finish of a sentence that spans a page break. To activate this function, double-click on the space between pages.

This is only a taste of the dozens of formatting and organization options available in Word. When you read a document prepared with an earlier version of Word or when you import documents from other formats, you have dozens of options for preserving the imported format or adjusting to Word's preferred formatting.

Here's another Excel sample. If your worksheet contains a list of people with their first names in one column and their last names in another, you can easily create a column with each person's first and last names in each cell. Begin by typing the first person's first and last names in the first cell of an empty column. When you continue to the next cell and begin typing the second person's first and last name, Excel will offer to complete the entire column with the first and last names of everyone else on the list automatically. That is a clever and convenient productivity feature.

Additionally, Excel provides explicit feedback prior to implementing an automatic function. When you Autosum a column of figures, for example, Excel displays the formula that will be used in the current cell. Alternatively, when you use the preceding technique to combine first and last names in a single column, Excel displays the combined names in gray and allows you to pause the process.

Excel's charting tool is capable of handling large amounts of data and provides subtle color palettes, in contrast to the gaudy colors utilized by older spreadsheet applications.

Excel incorporates a plethora of third-party extensions and features that enable it to execute specialized functions. For instance, a new Money in Excel tool works in conjunction with the Plaid service to make personal money management simple.

PowerPoint is the only presentation app that is feature-wise similar to Apple's KeyNote. As with its predecessor, PowerPoint enables you to manage and edit videos directly within the program, without the need for a separate video editor. Additionally, it enables you to incorporate online films into your presentations. As with KeyNote, you might lose track of time customizing transitions and other subtle changes in PowerPoint. For people who do not operate in the Apple universe, PowerPoint is our top recommendation for creating spectacular effects on a desktop-based presentation.

Automated Functions and Unbeknownst Complexities

However, some of Word's automated features can be vexing. For instance, you may wish to avoid Word formatting ordinals (the letters that follow the numbers in the first and second columns), but Word superscripts them automatically unless you backspace over the ordinal number and input it again. To disable this automated feature, you must have sufficient knowledge of Word to navigate to the Options > Proofing > AutoCorrect Options > AutoFormat section. This is not something that the majority of ordinary users will notice. Word also has certain poor habits, such as inserting horizontal lines after a succession of hyphens—another automated formatting quirk that requires numerous steps to disable. The enormous Options menu in Word provides an overview of the thousands of choices available for customizing the way Word produces and manages files.

When you utilize World's powerful Styles function, which allows you to select a collection of layout and formatting options that can be simply applied to a portion of text, you'll notice that Word occasionally, but not always, removes existing formatting (such as italics) when you apply a style. In these circumstances, Word appears to be unpredictable. This is mostly due to Microsoft's failure to document the principles it employs when applying styles. For example, when applying a style, Word will erase any current formatting that affects more than 50% of the text in the paragraph. I know this only because it was whispered to me years ago by an unidentified source deep within Microsoft.

Throughout Word's nearly four-decade history, many of its most powerful and widely exhibited capabilities have gradually been removed from the user interface, but remain accessible to advanced users who know where to look. For instance, Word was the first to incorporate variables into fields. If you create a field called BookTitle for the title of your book, you can use it in place of the actual title throughout your document. If you subsequently decide to alter the title, for example, from War and Peace to Captain Underpants, you can simply adjust the field's content to reflect the change. This feature is not available in the ribbon toolbar in the current version of Word; however, the help system indicates which keystrokes to use to handle it.

Mail and Web Applications

Outlook manages to cram all of its numerous functions into a small container, although it might feel a little overwhelming at times. Personally, I favor leaner applications like the open-source Thunderbird, commercial newcomers such as Mailbird on Windows, and Apple Mail on the Mac. Even the built-in Mail app in Windows 10 has certain advantages. However, for business use, Outlook's centralized interface for managing email, calendars, and contacts provides power and flexibility that competitors lack.

Outlook's UI can appear to have as many controls as the instrument panel of a large jet, but it places a massive number of capabilities within easy reach.

Microsoft's browser-based apps stand out for their elegance and usability, even topping Google's Workspace suite's basic design. Microsoft's programs, like Google's, allow you to dictate text through a microphone or transcribe text from an existing recording. Microsoft's voice-to-text capability worked really well for me when using mobile apps on a phone or tablet, but I was never able to get it to work inside a desktop or laptop browser on either a Mac or a Windows PC.

I had countless issues even accessing my Office documents using the majority of browsers on either a Windows or a Mac computer. I could open and modify the files in Firefox or Safari, but Chrome and Microsoft's Edge browsers reported that they couldn't locate the external files' addresses. This appears to be a long-standing issue, and before committing to using Office via a browser, you should determine whether you are experiencing the same issue.

Both Microsoft 365 and Google Workspace provide real-time collaboration via a browser in a similar fashion, with plenty of visual signals indicating what your colleagues are up to. If you keep your papers in OneDrive, Microsoft enables you to collaborate with colleagues on the desktop apps and take advantage of all of their ease and power. Google Workspace is incapable of matching this capability. In comparison, LibreOffice includes collaborative tools solely in its Calc spreadsheet, but not in real-time.

Mobile Access to Microsoft 365

The mobile versions of Microsoft's basic Word, Excel, and PowerPoint applications are surprisingly robust and attractive. If you don't want to clog your phone with the complete feature sets of the individual mobile apps, you may download a consolidated iPhone app called Office that has the essential capabilities of the individual apps.

If you're looking for Office software for your phone, consider the all-in-one Office app, which supports documents, workbooks, and presentations.

The individual mobile apps—of which I tested just the iOS versions—feel like native mobile applications, not shrunken clones of the PC applications. They have more comprehensible user interfaces than Google's competitors. Additionally, the Microsoft programs have a number of useful features that I enjoy on the desktop, such as a Welcome Back banner that informs me of my current location when I last saved a file and the ability to export in several formats.

Mobile Outlook and OneNote round out the offerings, but you may also want to check out Microsoft Lens, a mobile scanning and OCR application that enables you to photograph text and insert it into an office document using your camera. When I took images of books, I had inconsistent results, but it was better than nothing, and the seamless interface with Word and Excel is a significant benefit.

New Name, Same Superiority

Microsoft's Office applications are unmatched in their field. If you want to share editable documents with others, you'll almost definitely want to transmit them in a format compatible with Microsoft's apps—a logical method to assure that they can be edited by others. The one significant flaw I discovered with Microsoft's suite was the intermittent online access I encountered when testing on a variety of browsers.

For many years, I've used Microsoft Office applications on my desktop, laptop, and mobile devices. If you need to complete significant work in documents or spreadsheets, Microsoft's suite is not only worth the money, but an incredible value. Google's Workspace is another excellent option for people and enterprises who prefer a cloud-first approach to document editing.

Microsoft Store

The Microsoft Store is Windows users' default marketplace for downloading programs, games, TV shows, and movies. The upgrade to Windows 11 brings a redesigned interface with clearer categories and simplified navigation, making it easier to access the apps and media you need.

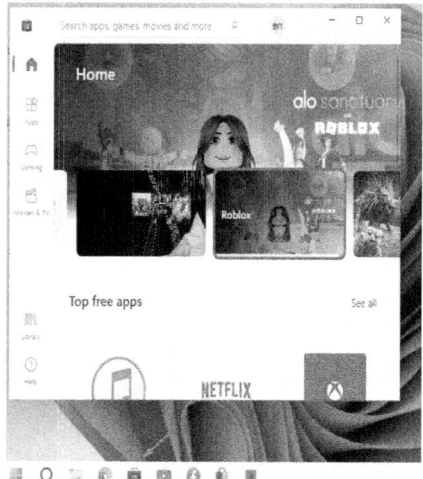

Additionally, Microsoft is making a significant step forward by making third-party stores available for download from the Microsoft Store. The Epic Games Store is the first to be introduced, offering a diverse selection of games and apps. The Amazon Appstore is currently in testing, allowing Android apps to run natively on Windows 11.

Use the Microsoft Store to navigate

To access the storefront on your Windows 11 PC, click the Microsoft Store icon in the taskbar. On the main screen, categories for promoted apps, essential apps, free games, top free apps, trending apps, and collections are displayed. Additionally, the Microsoft Store is divided into tabs for apps, games, and movies, and television series.

On the left sidebar, click the Apps icon to view available free and paid apps. Special deals, best-selling apps, productivity, and collections are all highlighted on the page.

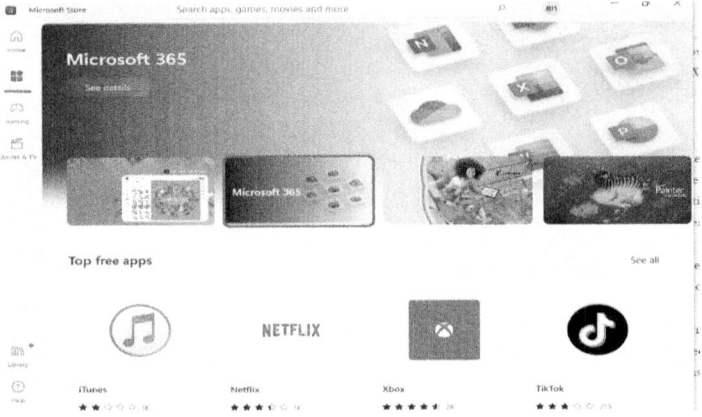

On the left, click the Gaming button and scroll down the screen to discover available free and paid games for download. The page features promoted games, best-selling games, top-rated free games, top-rated premium games, and collections.

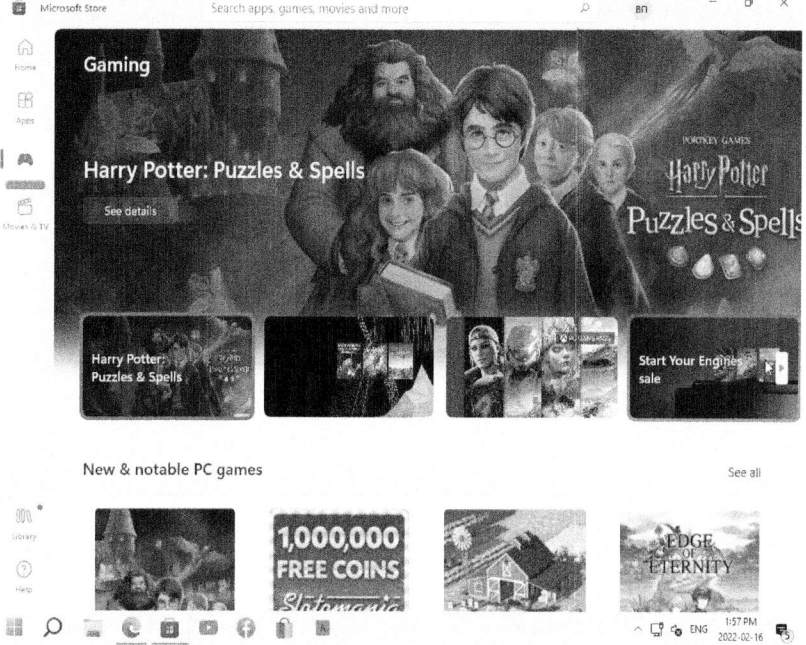

Are you looking to catch a film or a television show? On the left sidebar, click the Movies & TV icon. You can scroll down the screen to view new releases, featured releases, new television shows, top-rated television shows, and collections of films and television series.

Store Locator

Rather than looking through specific categories, you may simply search for an app, game, film, or television show. In the top search bar, enter your search word. You may then refine your search by picking from the Apps, Games, Movies, or TV Shows categories.

Numerous other parameters can be used to refine searches. You can filter by age group and type by clicking the Filters option at the upper right (free, paid, or on sale). You should be able to filter by additional parameters, such as category or subscription type, depending on the department you select.

Organize Library

Have you discovered something you'd want to download? Choose the desired application. If it is available for free, click the Get button. To access paid applications, click the button with the price displayed.

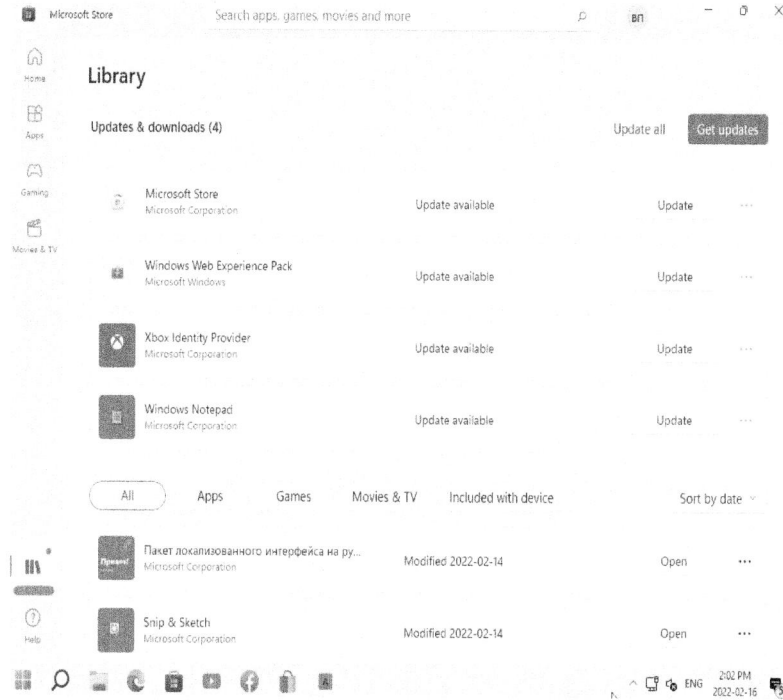

To keep track of the goods you've downloaded or purchased, click the Library button in the left sidebar's bottom-right corner. To launch a specific app, click the Open button next to it. To share the program, pin it to the taskbar, or add it to the Start menu, click the ellipsis button.

To obtain the most recent updates for your programs, click the Get Updates option. If the app has a cloud icon next to it, this indicates that it was downloaded from a different computer or device. To download it to your current device, click that icon. Additionally, you can sort the list of programs by date, name, installed status, or not installed status.

Epic Games Store - Download

The Microsoft Store will eventually feature storefronts from third-party developers, starting with the Epic Games Store and Amazon Appstore. Within the Microsoft Store, look for and download the Epic Games Store app.

After installation, the Epic Games Store launcher appears on the desktop and on the Start menu's App List screen. Open the program and log in using an Epic Games, Facebook, Google, Xbox Live, or Apple account.

The Epic Games Store mostly sells PC games, some of which are available for free. To download and install a commercial game, click the price button; to download and install a free game, click the Get button. Additionally, there are non-gaming applications such as the Brave browser, Discord, iHeartRadio, and Spotify.

To view all your games and apps, click the Library button, and then click an entry to install or launch it. To manage your Epic Games apps and downloads, select Settings. From there, you may enable or disable certain features such as offline browsing and cloud saves.

Configure the Microsoft Store Account

To manage all of your Microsoft Store apps, devices, and accounts, click your profile icon and then select Manage account and devices to access the Microsoft account management website. You can cancel or renew memberships, as well as view and unlink any linked devices, from this page.

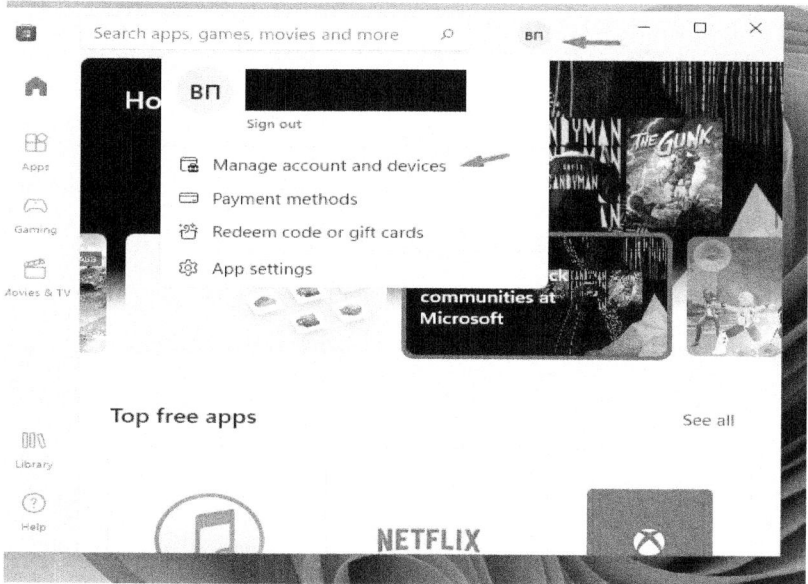

To configure or manage your payment method for Microsoft Store purchases, click your profile symbol and then select Payment methods. Following that, you can view your transactions and add or remove a payment method.

To redeem a coupon code or gift card in-store, click your profile symbol and then select Redeem coupon code or gift cards. Enter the gift card or coupon number and redeem the code at the window.

To access your app's settings, click on your profile symbol and then on App settings. You may next specify whether apps should be updated automatically, if Microsoft should prompt you for a password when you make a purchase, whether the current PC should run apps and games when it is not connected to the Internet, and whether autoplay should be enabled or disabled.

How to install Windows 11's new Microsoft Store application

Microsoft recently released the first public preview of Windows 11 for developers and enthusiasts, which included a slew of new features and improvements, such as a redesigned Start menu and updated taskbar with centered alignment, the next evolution of Action Center, an updated version of File Explorer, and a newly redesigned Microsoft Store app.

However, it appears as though there has been some confusion among Windows Insider Program participants over the new Store, as some users have reported that after downloading Windows 11, the preview of the new app is missing.

If you run into this issue, it is not because Microsoft is restricting access to the Store's first preview. The misunderstanding here is that this Windows preview does not include the program pre-installed. If the program was not updated automatically, you must download it manually using the legacy version of the Store.

Follow these instructions to obtain a sample of the new Microsoft Store app on Windows 11:

- Launch the traditional Microsoft Store.
- Select the Downloads and updates option by clicking the See more (three-dotted) button.
- To receive updates, click the Get updates button.

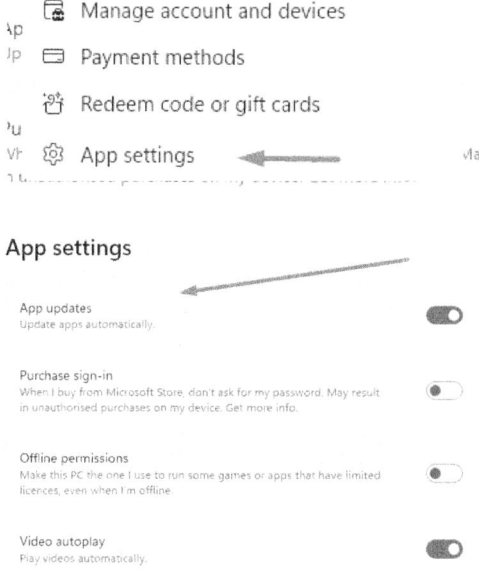

43

Once you've completed these steps, the system will check for updates to all installed programs, including those from the Microsoft Store. The Store app will close automatically throughout this procedure, and the next time you open it, you should see the updated experience.

Allow automatic updates to the Store

To ensure that future updates are downloaded immediately as they become available, set the Microsoft Store to automatically update apps.

To modify the new Microsoft Store's update settings, follow these steps:

- Launch the traditional Microsoft Store.
- Select the App settings to option from the profile menu.
- Switch on the toggle switch for App updates.

Once you've completed the steps, apps and future updates to the new Microsoft Store app should automatically install.

If a new feature is released for the Store and you do not see it, repeat the previous procedures. Additionally, you may verify the version on the "Apps settings" tab to ensure you have the most recent version installed.

Apart from the built-in features of Windows 11, the Microsoft Store has been enhanced to include thousands of third-party apps that extend the capabilities of the operating system and address additional demands. Previously, the Windows Store supported only Universal Windows Apps; however, it now offers classic desktop applications such as Canva, WinZip, and Zoom.

When you initially install Windows 11, it can be overwhelming to choose your first programs from the colossal amount of apps available in the all-new Microsoft Store. Additionally, it is frequently difficult to obtain all essential applications without a specific list. That is why I am going to compile a list of all the critical applications you must install on Windows 11 – right here.

Be Focused

The Pomodoro technique is a time management approach that utilizes a timer to divide work into 25-minute intervals separated by 5-minute pauses.

Because it is known to promote productivity, Be Focused assists you in implementing the Pomodoro technique in order to maintain focus and increase productivity. Additionally, you can tailor the duration of work and breaks to your own requirements.

OneNote

OneNote is a digital notebook application that assists you in organizing your notes on your Windows PC. On OneNote, you can scribble down ideas and type, write or draw, or capture web pages.

You may easily share your notes in real time with friends and family and across platforms. Additionally, you may download OneNote for Android and iOS if you want to access your notes on the road from multiple devices.

Microsoft To Do

Microsoft To Do is one of the best productivity tools available. To Do is a simple-to-use application that allows you to organize your tasks across all of your devices. On the To Do app, under My Day, you may arrange your entire day in a personalized manner.

Additionally, you may share your chores in real time with friends and family or create group assignments to complete with others. With a few clicks, you may divide jobs down into steps or customize the design with bold colors to increase focus.

LibreOffice

If you're not interested in paying for Office 365 and prefer an offline office, LibreOffice is the best option. It is an open-source, offline office suite that simplifies the process of creating documents, spreadsheets, and presentations. However, when dealing with complex issues, it can be a little more hazy than Microsoft Office.

PhaseExpress

PhaseExpress is a text expansion tool that comes in useful when you're typing material for hours on end. It aids in the acceleration of writing in any program, including email clients, text editors, and web browsers.

It expands text using textual shortcuts or hotkeys. Additionally, its template manager enables you to build and change text expansions in a variety of languages and categories.

Google Chrome

Chrome is a browser that every Windows PC should have. Google Chrome automatically syncs your browser history, saved passwords, and favorite sites across all of your devices, allowing you to take your browsing with you wherever you go.

Chrome not only generates and saves secure passwords, but also alerts you to online security breaches, thereby assisting you in safeguarding your privacy. One of its most useful features is that you may get solutions to math computations, dictionary searches or word definitions, and weather forecasts directly from the address cum search bar.

Mozilla Firefox

Along with Google Chrome and Microsoft Edge, Firefox is one of the most popular web browsers. It advertises itself as a lightning-fast browser while putting a premium on privacy-related features, as it does not collect information about your surfing activity. It also contains intriguing features similar to Chrome, such as picture-in-picture mode, dark mode, and theming support.

Skype

Skype is one of the most widely used video conferencing and messaging applications. It has capabilities such as one-to-one and group audio and video calling, call recording, live subtitles, smart messaging, and screen sharing.

Though Microsoft is emphasizing Teams in Windows 11, this app is required if you use Skype. It's an excellent substitute for Microsoft Teams when it comes to communicating with friends and family.

Franz

Franz is a multi-channel communication platform that integrates with dozens of personal and business messaging apps, including WhatsApp, Facebook Messenger, Slack, Messenger, and WeChat.

What's more, you may add several accounts for the same service and create distinct workspaces for business and personal accounts, and you'll only receive notifications from those accounts.

WhatsApp For Windows PC

With billions of active users, WhatsApp is the most popular messaging program. The desktop version of WhatsApp is useful if you don't want to constantly check your phone while working on your computer. As with the smartphone app, you can monitor your chats, receive notifications when new messages arrive, and send messages.

Outlook

Outlook is a critical application – especially for professionals. Outlook by Microsoft consolidates your emails and calendar into a single window on Windows 11. Additionally, it simplifies access to many email accounts, such as your business email, personal email, and so on.

While it has a web version, its desktop program provides faster access to your inbox via email notifications.

Microsoft News

If you're looking for a stylish way to keep up with the news, Microsoft News is the app for you. It's a wonderful, free app that provides you with a customised news stream. It personalizes your experience according to your chosen interests and themes.

It gathers news from a variety of sources, allowing you to select the news sources from which you want to read, and Microsoft News will display only news from those sources.

Discord

If you're a gamer, Discord is an absolute must-have. Discord – Slack for gamers — enables you to communicate with your other gamers and guild members via voice calls or text conversations.

There are dozens of groups dedicated to specific games, websites, or hobbies. You may connect with individuals who share your interests and organize your next raid or host an online event for everyone to enjoy.

Media Player VLC

If you don't mind a little hyperbole, VLC is a miracle media player. The reason for this is that VLC can play virtually any media file thrown at it. It produces the highest-quality images of any video — even on less-than-stellar hardware.

Additionally, VLC has useful capabilities such as video conversion, playing from a network stream, and putting a video as the backdrop wallpaper.

Notepad++

Notepad++ is a free text editor for source code that supports a variety of languages. Notepad++ includes built-in functionality for sophisticated search and macros, as well as the ability to work on multiple documents concurrently.

One of the best features of Notepad++ is that, unlike some other hefty IDEs, it takes very little processing power, making it an excellent choice for developers using older PCs.

Ditto Clipboard

Ditto Clipboard is a plug-in for the built-in Windows Clipboard that provides some extremely useful capabilities. Ditto Clipboard enables you to retrieve previously saved data.

You can save data that the clipboard supports, such as text and photos. While the all-new Windows Clipboard also allows you to paste old data, Ditto allows you to go further back in time than the Clipboard.

PC Decrapifier

PC Decrapifier is the software of your dreams that will rescue you from the nightmare of removing a device-critical application. Additionally, it is recommended that you uninstall bloatware or superfluous applications from your Windows PC. Having stated that, it fulfills this dual purpose, assisting in providing a seamless experience.

Wiztree

Wiztree is another utility program that instantly displays the amount of disk space consumed by each application or file. It assists you in visually locating and deleting massive stray files, such as a movie copied to the wrong folder or a temporary file taking up a large amount of space on your hard drive, hence assisting you in freeing up space.

Google Drive

Google Drive is a cloud storage service that provides 15 GB of cloud storage for uploading files, documents, and photographs and syncing them across all of your devices.

Additionally, you may share files and folders directly from Drive with your friends and family. Additionally, following a recent upgrade, it now allows you to grant access to a folder to a single account while banning access to the folder for unauthorized users.

Dropbox

Dropbox is another cloud storage provider that can be used to create a modern work environment. It enables you to collaborate with your team and securely access all of your files and folders in one location.

With a few clicks, you may save up space on your device by using its cloud storage or share a large file with your peers.

DC Acrobat Reader

A PDF reader is a must-have for your Windows PC, and Adobe Acrobat Reader DC is the best PDF reader available. Acrobat Reader enables you to view, sign, collaborate on, and annotate PDF files.

Additionally, it enables you to rapidly convert files between formats and search through several files simultaneously.

Wallpaper Studio

If you're sick of your Windows PC's default wallpaper, it's time to download Wallpaper Studio from the Microsoft shop. It gives you access to thousands of wallpapers for your desktop.

Additionally, the program enables you to make personalized wallpapers from your images and/or movies.

Code Writer

If you're a developer in need of a text and code editor, Code Writer is an incredible program. It supports over 20 different file types, and its fast and fluid interface makes it ideal for editing text files and doing code reviews, among other things. Additionally, it has convenient features like a search bar, document explorer, and print tool.

Zoom

Due to the pandemic, video conferencing software has become an integral part of life — even more so in this age of distant work. Zoom is one of the best video conferencing software for Windows PCs since it includes a number of features such as group calling, screen sharing, and chat.

Your Phone

Using the Your Phone app, you may connect your Android phone to your PC. Microsoft's Your Phone enables you to stay on top of your life by allowing you to receive texts and messages on your PC in real time. You can send and receive messages, make and receive calls, and use your phone apps directly from your PC.

Bot Converter

Another free application that is a must-have with Windows 11 is Convertor Bot. It enables one-click conversion of one format to another, allowing you to open and/or play any file format – even if your machine does not support it. The reason for this is that it supports hundreds of file formats and enables you to preview and convert them.

Malwarebytes

Malwarebytes is a highly effective application for identifying and eliminating malware. It includes specific anti-ransomware, anti-virus, and spyware removal capabilities.

Malwarebytes protects both business and personal users with its extensive information security capabilities.

Wox

While Windows has always made it simple to find applications and files, Wox takes the experience to the next level. Wox is an open-source application launcher that simplifies the process of searching for applications and files spread around your system. Additionally, it facilitates web searching: simply type your search query inside Wox.

Chapter 2: Security settings

Whichever version of Windows 11 you choose, you'll need to understand what security features are incorporated and available so you can adopt it successfully across your organization. Early evidence indicates promise: the new Windows 11 features have reduced malware on tested machines by 60%.

Consider the security features that businesses may expect from Windows 11 and the standards that they must meet.

While Windows 10 had security capabilities such as virtualization-based security (VBS), enterprises were required to activate them manually. However, these functionalities will be enabled by default in Windows 11—one of the reasons for the increased CPU requirements. This is part of Microsoft's much-needed move toward making security less optional.

Several of the following features will be enabled by default in Windows 11:

- Execution control depending on the VBS mode (ensures optimal performance while VBS is running)
- Encryption of the trusted platform module (TPM)
- Secure boot Hypervisor-based code integrity protection (HVCI)
- Data Protection in the Windows Sandbox Kernel (KDP)

Prepared for Zero Trust

Microsoft touts Windows 11 as being "zero trust ready" due to the inclusion of these security technologies. This should reduce the amount of incidents that cybersecurity professionals must investigate, hence boosting reaction time. Additionally, Windows 11 enables the determination of whether or not a device has security features enabled, much like how someone today might utilize their immunization card. Before gaining access to data, a device must demonstrate its security, just as you might be required to produce your vaccination card to enter a musical venue.

When combined with the OS's out-of-the-box support for Microsoft Azure Attestation (MAA), Windows 11 provides both software- and hardware-based zero trust protection. MAA is capable of confirming the integrity of hardware or software attempting to access sensitive cloud resources remotely. It is vital for organizational scalability to extend protection to both cloud and on-premises systems.

Virtualization

One of the improvements promised by Windows 11 was support for Android applications, which required application virtualization. Because development on mobile devices would be incredibly challenging, developers require a mechanism to execute the program from their PCs. They can use virtualization to test software features on their PC before releasing them to the public.

VBS leverages hardware virtualization to protect security features and prevent malware from infecting them, even if the rest of the device is compromised.

Microsoft intends to operate virtualization in the future via individual Krypton containers. While Microsoft has made this functionality available for Windows 10X, it is not yet included in Windows 11.

Sandboxing

Windows Sandbox enables users to run applications in a separate, secure environment from the rest of their computer. When the user exits the application, the sandbox is removed. This stops potentially malicious apps from accessing other files and applications on the device.

While Microsoft did not anticipate home consumers being interested in sandboxing, they have observed significant interest. Because sandboxing alters the experience of running a program, Microsoft is still attempting to strike a balance between security and usability.

Access Without a Password

Windows Hello eliminates the need for passwords on your devices, instead of relying on a PIN, fingerprint, or facial recognition. Passwordless access will be enabled by default for consumers, but enterprises will be able to implement basic passwordless models. Additionally, IT managers will have granular control over authentication techniques in order to guarantee that users adhere to company policies.

Along with greater security, passwordless access can help IT teams save money by reducing the amount of time spent assisting users with password resets. And, given that 81 percent of breaches involve the use of stolen or compromised passwords, this means that IT will have fewer resources to devote to tracking down intruders.

As it turns out, all of these capabilities are already included in the 20H2 edition of Windows 10. (Windows 10 October 2020 Update). As a consumer, small business, or corporate, you can take advantage of these features by deploying Group Policy or by turning them on directly from the Device Security menu in Windows 10. You are not required to wait for the introduction of Windows 11 or to purchase a new PC.

TPM 2.0 and Secure Boot are the first features.

The Trusted Platform Module (TPM) is a security-related cryptographic function that is implemented in hardware. If your PC was created within the last five years, the chances are that it includes a TPM chip that supports version 2.0. This information can be obtained by opening Device Manager and expanding "Security devices." You're set to go if it says "Trusted Platform Module 2.0."

Enumeration of Microsoft Windows Device Manager with TPM 2.0

This is referred to as the "Security Processor" in Windows 10's Device Security Settings menu (and Windows 11).

So, what exactly does TPM do? It is used to generate and store cryptographic keys that are specific to your system, such as an RSA encryption key that is specific to your system's TPM. TPMs are utilized to facilitate the Secure Boot procedure in addition to their traditional application with smart cards and VPNs. It verifies the integrity of the operating system's boot code, including firmware and individual operating system components, to ensure they have not been tampered with.

There is nothing you need to do to make it work; it just does, as long as your UEFI does not deactivate it. Secure Boot on Windows 10 can be deployed via Group Policy or a corporate MDM solution such as Microsoft Endpoint Manager.

While the majority of manufacturers ship their PCs with TPM enabled, some may disable it; therefore, if it is not shown in Device Manager or is disabled, boot into your UEFI firmware settings and check.

If your system's TPM has never been configured for use, simply run tpm.msc from the command line.

Virtualization-Based Security (VBS) and Hypervisor-Based Control Interface (HVCI)

While TPM 2.0 has been a standard feature on many PCs for over six years, the feature that truly puts the security rubber on the road in Windows 10 and Windows 11 is HVCI, or Hypervisor-Protected Code Integrity, also known as Memory Integrity or Core Isolation in the Windows Device Security menu.

While Windows 11 requires it, Windows 10 requires it to be enabled manually. Simply click on "Core Isolation Details" and toggle Memory Integrity on. Your system may take up to a minute to turn it on, since it must inspect each memory page in Windows before activating it.

This capability is available only on 64-bit CPUs that support hardware-based virtualization extensions such as Intel's VT-X or AMD's AMD-V. While they were first developed in 2005 in server-class CPUs, they have been included in almost all desktop computers since at least 2015, or Intel Generation 6. (Skylake). However, it requires Second Level Address Translation (SLAT), which is included in Intel's Virtualization Technology X2 with Extended Page Tables (EPT) and AMD's Rapid Virtualization Indexing (RVI).

Additionally, HVCI mandates that every I/O device capable of Direct Memory Access (DMA) be positioned behind an IOMMU (Input-Output Memory Management Unit). These instructions are implemented in CPUs that enable Intel VT-D or AMD-Vi.

While this may appear to be a lengthy list of criteria, the basic line is that if Device Security reports that these functionalities are present on your system, you are ready to go.

Isn't virtualization mostly used to increase the density of workloads on datacenter servers or by software developers to isolate their testing environment on their workstations or to run foreign operating systems such as Linux? True, however virtualization and containerization/sandboxing are increasingly being employed in modern operating systems, including Windows, to provide extra security levels.

In Windows 10 and Windows 11, VBS, or Virtualization-based Security, creates and isolates a secure memory zone from the operating system using Microsoft's Hyper-V. This protected region is used to execute many security solutions that can protect the operating system from legacy vulnerabilities (such as those caused by out-of-date application code) and prevent attacks that seek to circumvent those protections.

HVCI leverages VBS to bolster code integrity policy enforcement by verifying all kernel-mode drivers and binaries prior to startup and blocking the loading of unsigned drivers and system files into system memory. These restrictions safeguard critical operating system resources and security assets such as user credentials; thus, even if malware gains access to the kernel, the scope of an exploit can be limited and contained due to the supervisor's ability to prevent the malware from executing code or accessing secrets.

VBS also verifies application code prior to loading and begins them only if they are signed by approved code signers, which it accomplishes by assigning rights over every page of system memory. All of this occurs within a secure memory zone, which offers enhanced protection against kernel viruses and malware.

Consider VBS as Windows' new code enforcement officer, your kernel and applications acting as Robocop in a protected memory box enabled by your virtualized CPU.

Microsoft Defender Application Guard is a third feature (MDAG)

Microsoft Defender Application Guard is a function that many Windows users are unfamiliar with (MDAG).

This is another virtualization-based technology (affectionately known as "Krypton" Hyper-V containers) that, when combined with the latest Microsoft Edge (and, via an extension, with current versions of Chrome and Firefox), creates an isolated memory instance of your browser, preventing your system and enterprise data from being compromised by untrusted websites.

Should the browser get contaminated with scripting or malware, the Hyper-V container, which operates independently of the host operating system, isolates the infected browser from essential system operations and company data.

MDAG is used in conjunction with the Network Isolation settings configured for your environment to define the boundaries of your private network according to the enterprise's Group Policy.

MDAG's operation on the host computer and the isolated Hyper-V browser container.

MDAG can also be used in conjunction with Microsoft 365 and Office to prohibit Word, PowerPoint, and Excel documents from accessing trusted resources such as enterprise credentials and data. This functionality was made available to Microsoft 365 E5 customers in August 2020 as part of a Public Preview.

MDAG is included in the Windows 10 Professional, Enterprise, and Educational SKUs and may be enabled using the Windows Features menu or a simple PowerShell command; it is not dependent on Hyper-V being enabled.

11 Security settings you should know

Microsoft requires that computers equipped with a Trusted Platform Module (TPM) 2.0 component integrated into the motherboard qualify for the Windows 11 upgrade, demonstrating the company's commitment to security on its new systems. talking.

TPM 2.0 is a security mechanism that confirms the user's identity and safeguards data against attack. Among other safeguards, TPM makes it extremely difficult for someone who is not seated in front of a Windows machine to gain access.

However, the Trusted Platform Module is only the beginning of Microsoft's security and privacy protections integrated into Windows 11. If you recently installed the new operating system on your computer, these are the security settings you should be aware of.

To begin, click on the button to bring up the Settings screen in Windows 11. menu Start Or abort button On the resulting panel, click More in the taskbar Adjustment section.

1. Maintain Windows 11 Updates

Effective security begins with software updates, and by selecting Windows Update in Settings, you can view all of the most recent system upgrades and bug fixes. Select the advanced options. I have an active time period. To ensure that Windows does not restart or apply updates throughout the workday. We are explained how to do it earlier.

2. Examine Login Options

In the upper left corner of the Settings window, click your name, followed by the login option. To learn about the many methods for logging into a computer. If face recognition (using your webcam or a fingerprint sensor) or fingerprint recognition (using a fingerprint sensor) are available, they are more secure than passwords and should be supported by the majority of modern computers.

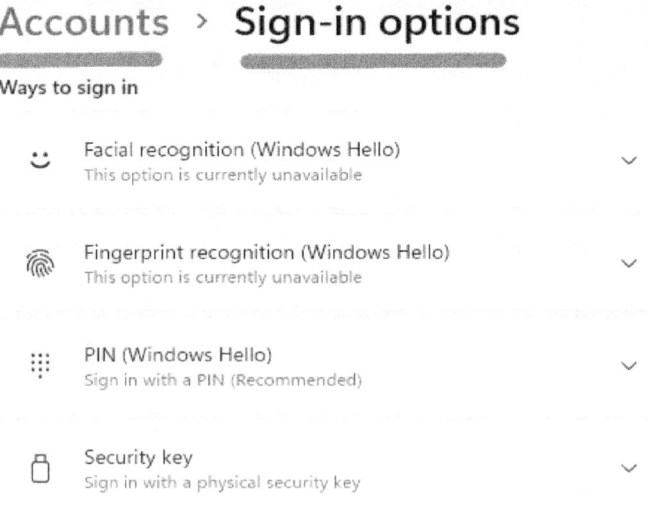

3. When You're Away, Log Out

When you leave a computer, use the logout button on the same login choices screen; this approach is also critical. Additionally, you may utilize the Dynamic Lock option to instruct Windows to lock your device when you leave it (as indicated by the location of the connected smartphone).

4. Enable Integrated Security Tools

If you click on Privacy & Security and then on Windows Security in Settings, you may check to see if the built-in security software is enabled. This is critical if you do not already have third-party settings installed. Any security concern requiring your attention will be indicated by a yellow exclamation point - click on it to view additional alert details.

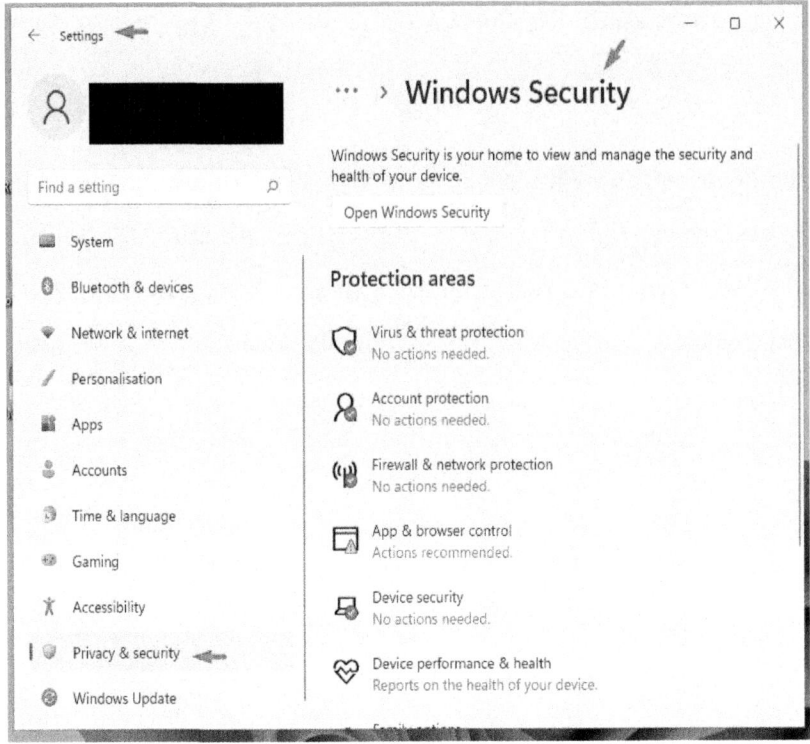

5. Conduct a Malware Scan

You can click open windows security from the same Windows Security screen. To gain access to the Integrated Security Center in Windows 11. While the majority of the functionality here should run in the background automatically, including scans for harmful viruses, you may also perform scans manually by selecting Protection. Select further fast scans for viruses and threats.

6. Verify the Device's Security

After opening Windows Security Tools, any hardware concerns with your Windows 11 computer — including TPM and Secure Boot process difficulties — will be noted in the security page device.

They will be listed if quick action is required to safeguard the operating system and stored data.

7. Keep Yourself Safe While Online

When you select Application & Browser Control in the Windows Security program, you'll notice two options: reputation-based protection (which means Windows 11 is always scanning for suspicious or poorly performing applications) and security exploits (which help mitigate the effects of various types of remote hacker attacks).

8. Examine the Safety Equipment You Possess

Abrasive security configurations Windows will display the software that protects your Windows 11 machine and security providers — this may be included security software or third-party solutions. Additionally, you can adjust security notification settings to ensure that you are notified at all times.

9. Manage Permissions for Applications

As with a smartphone, you can control the rights apps in Windows 11 can utilize. From the main screen, navigate to the Privacy & Security tab. Adjustment Continue scrolling down to view Additional Permissions. On the screen, click the rights you wish, such as Location, Camera, and Microphone.

10. Ascertain that your gadget can be located in the event it becomes lost.

Affix me Privacy & Security, then click Adjustment, then select Additional find my device. So that your location can be tracked on a periodic basis. This enables you to log into your Microsoft account from a different device and determine the location of your Windows 11 notebook.

11. Protect the data on your device by encrypting it.

Encrypting your hard drive's data makes it even more difficult for others to read it (for example, if they can eject the drive from your computer). This feature is not available on every machine, but if it is on yours, you can enable it by selecting Privacy & Security and then on-screen device encryption in the Windows 11 Settings.

What security software to install?

Obtaining a new operating system necessitates the acquisition of an antivirus tool capable of providing superior protection against viruses. When it comes to choosing an antivirus, comprehensive software that includes additional protection measures is what you need. Thus, the following points should be considered when selecting the best antivirus for Windows 11:

- Lab results from a non-profit organization. Certain labs conduct antiviral testing and disclose the results to determine how well a service defends against various threats. Usability, performance, and protection are all considered. When selecting an antivirus service, you can determine whether one is capable of effectively protecting your device.

- Efficiency. Antivirus software's routine background scans can consume significant amounts of memory and CPU. That is why you should choose a lightweight antivirus solution to ensure that your device is not clogged.

- Features. While some antivirus software are limited to scanning your device for infection, others offer additional features. For instance, parental controls that allow you to monitor your child's online activities or webcam protection that keeps you safe from prying eyes. Different services provide distinct advantages, and you should select the one that best suits your needs.

- Customer service. Due to the fact that you require protection for your device at all times, having access to customer assistance is a major benefit in the event that you encounter any troubles. Even if you just do not understand anything, you should be able to obtain assistance, all the more so if you have paid for the goods.

- Price. The most expensive antivirus service does not always mean it is the finest. Antivirus software can vary significantly in terms of malware detection rates and capabilities. You should consider your own particular requirements to ensure that you get your money's worth.

The best antivirus software for Windows 11 – a comprehensive list:

The following list contains only the best antivirus software for Windows 11. Additionally, it contains the benefits and drawbacks of each piece of software, allowing you to choose what is and is not a deal-breaker for you. Let us begin with the reviews.

Bitdefender Antivirus - the best antivirus for Windows 11 for everyone

Firewall: Yes

Version gratuit: Yes

Operating systems: Windows, macOS, Android, and iOS

Bitdefender may be less well-known than some other antivirus software – but it makes up for that with incredible performance, real-time protection, and other security features. Additionally, it features a free edition for individuals on a budget.

Bitdefender provides an Advanced Threat Defense solution that keeps track of all device processes. Additionally, the Ransomware Mitigation feature detects and removes ransomware from your device.

Additionally, anti-phishing and anti-spam filters, as well as webcam and microphone protection, are included in the security measures. Additionally, the bundle includes a password manager and a file shredder.

Bitdefender differs from other antivirus software in that it does not charge an additional fee for the VPN service. However, the VPN included with the package has a data cap. Another reason customers choose Bitdefender is that it adapts to the environment in which they are. It ensures that you are not interrupted when working or watching a movie by random pop-up notifications.

What I found intriguing is that customer support is open to all users, even those who are not paying. There is a live chat available 24 hours a day, an email address, and even a phone number for complete help. Prices are lower for first-time customers and gradually climb over the course of a year. While there are less expensive solutions available, Bitdefender provides more features and excellent, high-quality performance.

Pros

- Excellent performance on independent testing
- Numerous customer service possibilities
- Available Trial periods of 30 days
- Has a no-cost variant
- Notification settings are activity-dependent

Cons

- macOS is only supported on premium programs.
- Payment is required for full VPN access.
- Quite costly

Norton 360 Is a capable all-purpose antivirus program for Windows 11

Firewall: Yes

Version gratuit: No

There are no platforms available: Windows, macOS, Android, or iOS.

Norton is feature-rich and one of the best antivirus programs for Windows 11 currently available. However, despite the abundance of additional capabilities, it also performs admirably on the fundamentals, including excellent malware detection and real-time security. It is an all-in-one antivirus solution.

Norton employs artificial intelligence (AI) to identify any online threats. It safeguards your computer from malware, spyware, ransomware, and viruses. Additionally, it features the Norton Safe Web tool, which assists you in determining which links pose a risk of danger. If you must click on the malicious URLs for some reason, Norton includes an Isolation Mode. It assists in preventing injury even on dangerous websites.

Additionally, the Norton 360 subscriptions offer a Virtual Private Network (VPN) service called Norton Secure VPN. No third parties will be able to access your information or online activities if you use this tool. Norton also includes a two-way firewall. It keeps track of all network traffic delivered and received on your computer.

Norton antivirus is a good pick due to its high quality and extensive feature set. It's not difficult to learn how to use it, and if you run into any difficulties, a live chat function or a 24/7 hotline are available. Although it is rather expensive, it is well worth the money when you consider how efficient it is and how many useful features you receive.

Pros

- Protection on both sides
- Additional characteristics
- Interface that is simple to use
- Minimal resource consumption
- Protection against identity theft

Cons

- There is no free version included.
- Quite costly

Kaspersky Anti-Virus - superior antivirus protection

Firewall: Yes

Version gratuit: Yes

Operating systems: Windows, macOS, Android, and iOS

Kaspersky is a market veteran, and as such, there is little doubt that it performs admirably. And, while Kaspersky has been the subject of numerous speculations regarding their relationship, one thing is certain - this antivirus remains a great tool for protecting you against all types of online threats.

It achieved a perfect score of 100 percent in recent lab tests for capturing widespread malware. Additionally, the bundle includes a privacy security guard feature that informs you when someone attempts to collect your data. Additionally, there is a secure money facility that safeguards your online payment information.

As is the case with the majority of leading antivirus programs, Kaspersky includes a VPN powered by Hotspot Shield. It's quite simple, yet it's quite straightforward to use. The most expensive package comes with a password manager. Additionally, if you have children, you can follow the position of their smartphone to ensure their safety.

The installation procedure is straightforward and straightforward, as is the user interface. Kaspersky maintains a knowledge base for the most often encountered issues. Additionally, they give 24/7 technical help via phone, chat, and email. If you want to test the waters and see if you like this supplier, you can sign up for their basic free version.

Pros

- Outstanding anti-malware protection
- Excellent test results for autonomous organizations
- Interface that is simple to use
- Customer service alternatives available 24 hours a day
- There is a free version available.

Cons

- Reduced brand trust
- Quite costly
- Only on the most expensive plans is a password manager available.

How we chose and evaluated these antivirus applications

When selecting an item for which you are aware that you will be charged, you want to ensure that you win the jackpot. That is why we chose antivirus software that provides value for money. Here are the criteria we use to choose the best antivirus software for Windows 11:

- Rates of virus detection. We collect data regarding an antivirus's performance, protection, and usability from independent organizations. AV-TEST and AV-Comparatives are two examples. The best antivirus software should have a protection score of at least 98 percent and should be capable of detecting zero-day malware.

- Possessing a false positive record. Each day, new varieties of malware emerge, and an antivirus cannot possibly detect them all. However, it is critical to understand how the antivirus supplier handles false positives. We exclusively select antivirus software that is unobtrusive when browsing.

- Additional features. Certain additional features can be really beneficial. For instance, parental settings that prevent your children from accessing potentially harmful websites.

- Customer service. When you run into difficulties when using an antivirus, you want to obtain prompt assistance. The more help choices available, the faster the issue can be resolved.

- Price. We make an effort to select antivirus software that is reasonably priced. We assess additional tools, virus detection rates, and customer support.

Why do I require antivirus protection for Windows 11?

You require an antivirus for Windows 11 in order to safeguard yourself from a variety of threats and prying eyes. Therefore, a more pertinent inquiry would be... why don't you have an antivirus? And, to be serious, it depends on the kind of your everyday online activities.

Do you frequently visit dubious-looking websites or are you aware of how to spot them? To be sure, you wouldn't have to worry about what you clicked on if you had a trustworthy antivirus.

Additionally, you never know when your computer is going to become infected. Additionally, it is possible to download the incorrect sort of file when searching for a specific application. Even a friend may unintentionally give you an attachment containing a virus. That is why you could benefit from additional protection.

If you're like me and easily swayed by commercials, you'd benefit as well. An antivirus program can encrypt your payment information, preventing third parties from accessing it.

Additionally, if you are a parent, your primary worry is undoubtedly the safety of your children. Certain antivirus programs incorporate parental control and even location tracking functions.

Certain suppliers offer complimentary antivirus software or a 30-day money-back guarantee. I'd recommend downloading one of the various free antivirus programs or downloading their trial versions to see what all the fuss is about.

How can I install anti-virus software on my Windows 11 computer?

Antivirus installation is frequently a straightforward and quick operation. The following are the primary steps that apply to the majority of antivirus software:

1. Navigate to the service provider's official website.
2. Select a plan and complete the registration process.
3. Complete the payment process and purchase the product.
4. Save the installation file to your computer.
5. Continue following the directions until the installation is complete.
6. Open the application and log in, and voila! You can now perform a scan.

Is it possible to use a free antivirus program with Windows 11?

Yes - you are free to select any option that you believe best meets your needs. If you only require protection against the most frequent viruses and harmful websites, you can choose for a free antivirus.

Nonetheless, a high-quality antivirus program can give comprehensive real-time protection. Additionally, depending on the paid antivirus you select, you obtain additional functions.

At the end of the day, a free antivirus program is not the worst option. It is preferable to have some security layers than to have none. And who knows, you might discover that your online privacy is well worth investing in!

Chapter 3: Interface settings

What are taskbar settings?

Along with a brand-new Start menu, Windows 11 introduces a new version of the Taskbar. While it may look familiar from Windows 10, the new experience is significantly improved.

For instance, the new Taskbar is aligned in the center, features a revamped Start button, and includes new buttons for Search, Task View, Widgets, and Chat. Additionally, there are new animations for opening, minimizing, maximizing, and installing applications, and Microsoft continues to improve the system tray in numerous ways.

However, it is not all good news, since the new Windows 11 Taskbar loses a number of personalization options accessible in prior versions.

The Taskbar has been redesigned.

While the taskbar in Windows 11 may appear to be identical to that in prior versions, it is not. Similar to the Start menu, Microsoft has altered the experience in a number of positive (and negative) ways.

Although the new Taskbar is centered, you may always adjust its behavior to the left, as with earlier versions. Additionally, the interface is six pixels taller than the one included with Windows 10. Along with the center-aligned buttons, you'll notice a new Start logo button, as well as new buttons for Search, Task View, Widgets, and Chat. Cortana and My People have been removed from the experience entirely.

Additionally, Taskbar items such as tooltips, overflow menus, previews, and highlighting buttons now use the new rounded corner design style. When an app wants your attention, the flashing will become more modest; it will ultimately stop, and you will notice a new backplate with a light red tint and a red pill icon indicating the app requires your attention. If you're not a fan of one of the feature icons, you may disable it under Settings > Personalization > Taskbar.

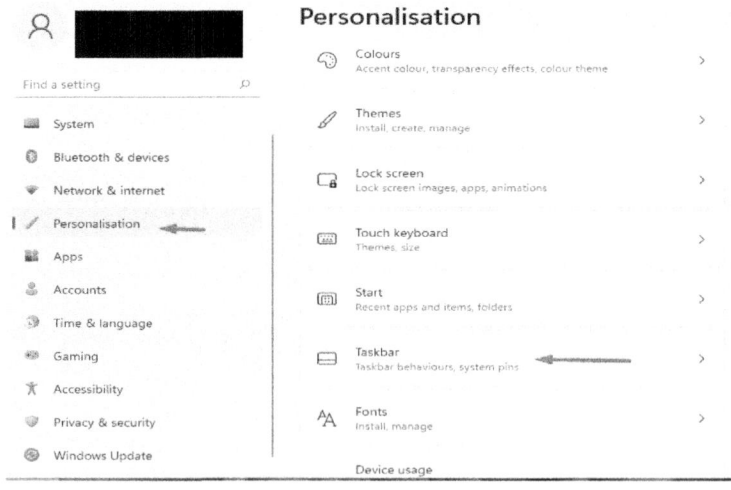

When you hover your cursor over the feature button, a fresh preview with some recent items or a brief look at the feature will show. When you hover over an open application, the thumbnail preview appears, just like it did in prior versions.

As part of the multitasking experience, when you use "Snap groups," you may now hover an app in the Taskbar, and if it is part of a snapped group, the experience will allow you to switch back to the snapped windows after switching to another app, eliminating the need to re-snap them. (While this functionality is shown in the Taskbar, the setting control for this behavior is accessible on the Multitasking settings page.)

The search box has been replaced in Windows 11 with the Search button, which launches Windows Search. The experience is nearly identical to that of Windows 10, with the addition of a search box at the top.

Additionally, the redesigned Taskbar has additional animations. For instance, when the device boots, you'll see a new bouncing motion when the Taskbar loads on the desktop. Additionally, there is a new little pill-shaped indication that changes size to indicate whether an application is minimized or maximized. Additionally, a new animation will appear when you click an app to open, minimize, or maximize it. Additionally, there is a new progress indicator for application installation.

Additionally, the system tray (bottom-right corner) is being improved. Windows has grouped the icons logically in this new version. For instance, the time and date, as well as the Focus help icon, are all part of a group. When you click it, a new "Notification Center" opens, which contains a full-month calendar and all of your alerts.

Then there's the group of symbols for the network, volume, and power. When you click it, the new Quick Settings experience opens, containing common settings such as volume, brightness, Wi-Fi, Bluetooth, Airplane mode, Night light accessibility, and Cast.

If you're using Microsoft Edge to watch a video or listen to music, the Quick settings will also display the media playback controls for controlling the stream.

Naturally, you can right-click any icon to open its settings or choose from the available alternatives.

Additionally, the context menu for the Taskbar has been updated to include simply one option to view the "Taskbar" settings page. On the settings page, you may add or remove items, customize the corner icons, and manage which apps appear in the overflow menu.

Additionally, in the Taskbar behaviors area, you may adjust the Taskbar's alignment, allow or disable app badges, enable or disable auto-hide, configure multiple displays, and even disable the show desktop button.

The new Taskbar's flaws

Along with the welcome enhancements, Microsoft is implementing other modifications that may give the impression that the Taskbar is regressing rather than progressing this time around.

One of the most bizarre changes is that the Taskbar is now fixed at the bottom of the screen and cannot be moved to the top or either side.

Only the Taskbar's icons can be displayed. If you are one of those who enjoy displaying labels and never combining apps, this is also no longer an option.

Additionally, Microsoft acknowledged that users will be unable to drag and drop files or apps to the Taskbar.

Additionally, in Windows 10 and previous versions, you could change the size of the icons. In this new version, there is just one icon size, and the opportunity to alter this behavior has been removed. Additionally, the Taskbar's height cannot be adjusted.

Although the system tray has some improvements, it may now be even more difficult to use due to the grouping of the icons and the inability to conceal the clock or any of the other system icons, such as volume, network, or microphone. If you wish to see the clock, the situation is made worse by the fact that it will not appear on secondary displays.

How to set up a desktop?

By default, Windows 11 does not display any unique icons on your desktop (such as "This PC" or "Recycle Bin"). If you want a more traditional Windows look, you may easily enable special desktop icons. This is how you do it.

To begin, right-click an empty space on the desktop and then select "Personalize" from the resulting menu.

The "Personalization" screen of the Windows Settings program will open. Select "Themes" from the list of Personalization categories.

Scroll down to "Desktop Icon Settings" in Themes.

The "Desktop Icon Settings" window will display. Place check marks beside the special icons you want to see on the desktop in the "Desktop Icons" area near the top of the window. For instance, if you want the Recycle Bin to appear on your desktop, check "Recycle Bin." When finished, click "OK."

The window will close after you click "OK." Additionally, you can close Settings. Consider your desktop; you'll see the distinctive icons that you enabled in the "Desktop Icon Settings" pane.

Tip: You can resize your desktop icons by holding down the Ctrl key on your keyboard and scrolling up or down with your mouse wheel.

If you change your mind and wish to hide particular special desktop icons, simply navigate to Settings > Personalization > Themes > Desktop Icon Settings and uncheck the icons you wish to hide.

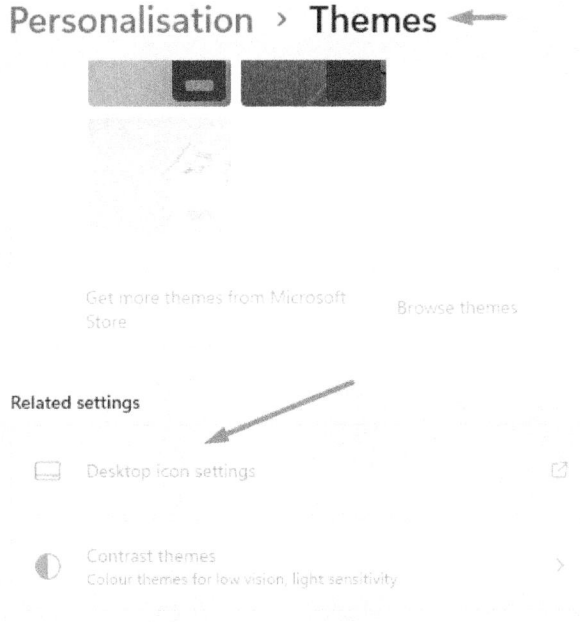

Rather than that, how about hiding all of your desktop icons? Simply right-click your desktop, navigate to "View," and toggle the option "Show Desktop Icons."

After that, you may like to continue customizing your desktop by changing the wallpaper.

What are Start Menu settings?

Before we do anything, let's have a look at the basic Windows 11 Start menu. A search area at the top of the menu allows you to look for apps, files, and settings. The Pinned area displays all pinned apps; scroll up and down to view them all. To get a list of all the applications you've installed, click the All Apps icon.

The Recommended area displays programs and files that have been recently installed or opened. To view a longer list, click the More button. Below this area is your profile icon, which allows you to modify account settings, lock the computer, and log out. The power button on the right allows you to put Windows to sleep, restart your computer, or shut it down completely.

Alternate Recommended Applications and Files

If you want to make any changes, navigate to Settings > Personalization > Start, where you can instruct Windows to disable the display of recently installed apps, commonly used apps, and recently used things in the Start menu, App List, and elsewhere. Experiment with all three of these options to determine which ones to activate and which ones to disable. If you disable all three choices, the Start menu's Recommended section will be empty.

Create Folders

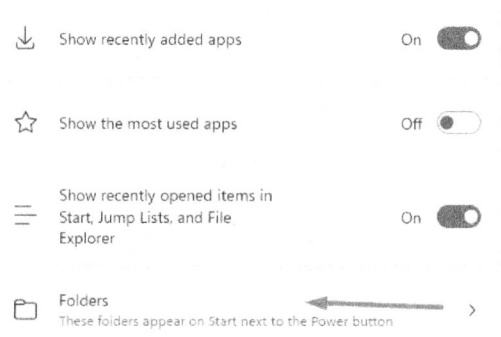

From Settings > Personalization > Start > Folders, you may add folders to the bottom of the Start menu. Next to the power symbol, turn on the switch next to any folder you desire to show. This provides convenient access to Settings, File Explorer, Documents, and Downloads, among other things.

Adding and Removing Pinned Applications

You can further customize the menu by deleting, pinning, and relocating individual apps under the Pinned area. To remove an app from the Start Menu, right-click its icon and select Unpin from Start. You'll notice that the app continues to appear in the App List.

To add an application to the Start menu, click All Apps to list all installed applications. Select Pin to Start from the context menu of an item that is not currently in the Start menu.

Any applications added to the Pinned area can be rearranged to your preference. Therefore, if you frequently utilize some more than others, pin them to the top of the Pinned area for easy access. To swiftly accomplish this, right-click the icon and select Move to Top. Alternatively, you may simply drag icons into place.

The Start Button should be realigned

Additionally, you may have noticed that the Start button is now centered on the taskbar in Windows 11, as opposed to its traditional location in the bottom-left corner of the screen. If you prefer the way the taskbar has always been positioned, you can reposition the entire taskbar.

Select the Taskbar behaviors option under Settings > Personalization > Taskbar. Change the icons' alignment from Center to Left using the Taskbar alignment drop-down. The Start button, as well as the rest of the Taskbar icons, will be repositioned to the bottom left.

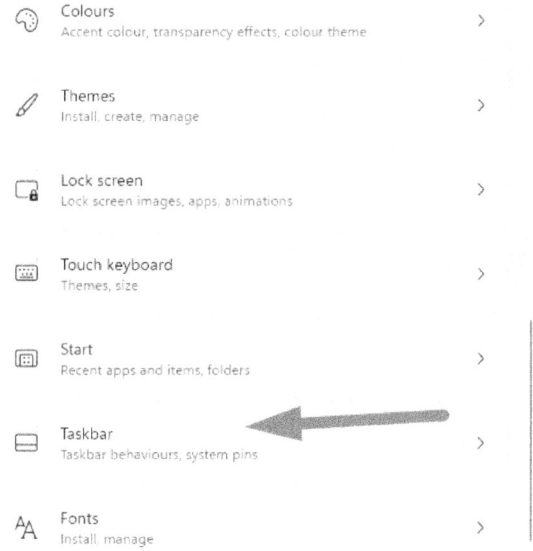

Personalisation

	Colours Accent colour, transparency effects, colour theme	>
	Themes Install, create, manage	>
	Lock screen Lock screen images, apps, animations	>
	Touch keyboard Themes, size	>
	Start Recent apps and items, folders	>
	Taskbar Taskbar behaviours, system pins	>
	Fonts Install, manage	>

Alternative to the Start Menu: Stardock's Start 11

If you remain dissatisfied with the Windows 11 Start menu, you may wish to explore downloading an alternative. A popular option is Stardock's Start 11, which is currently in beta but is available to everyone. For a free 30-day trial, visit Stardock.com and click the Download the current update link beneath the green Get the Beta icon. After that, it's $4.99 ($3.99 if you're upgrading from an earlier version) and includes 30 days of direct technical help, as well as unrestricted access to the company's tech support forums.

The program's setup screen prompts you to specify whether you want your taskbar to be left- or center-aligned. You can then select a Start menu style, such as Windows 7, Modern, Windows 10, or Windows 11. If you like the traditional two-column Start menu, choose Windows 7 or Modern. By clicking the down arrow next to a design, you can further customize it by selecting a compact or grid layout.

Proceed to the remaining configuration options to personalize the Start button, taskbar, and search feature. The Control tab allows you to customize when and how the Start 11 menu appears. For instance, you can configure it so that clicking the Start button launches the Start 11 menu, while pressing the Windows key on your keyboard launches the standard Windows 11 Start menu.

Once complete, click the Start button to view your newly created Start menu. Right-click anywhere on the Start menu to customize it by deleting or renaming shortcuts and relocating them to certain folders. Additionally, you may access the Start 11 settings by right-clicking the taskbar and selecting Configure Start 11.

Chapter 4: Manage your notifications

What is an Action Center?

Windows 11's Action Center is a critical component. It notifies users and also contains some useful settings. As a result, they frequently attempt to open the Action Center on Windows 11.

However, some of you may require assistance in resolving a few Action Center bugs in Windows 11. For instance, the Action Center's inability to open is one such issue.

When users are unable to access the Action Center, they are unable to change its settings or check for notifications. True, they can probably get by without it. However, there are a couple potential workarounds for the issue in Windows 11.

Why won't my Action Center open?

The identical issue with the Action Center not opening is present in Windows 10. When this occurs, the Action Center may be disabled in Windows 11.

Additionally, it is possible to disable it in Windows 11 Pro using certain Group Policy settings. Certain users confirmed that they required to modify their GPE policies to resolve the issue.

Alternatively, the problem could emerge as a result of corrupted or missing system files. In this instance, system file scanning may suffice. Another possibility is to restore the system.

When something goes wrong with the File Explorer process, it is also known to cause Action Center difficulties. Restarting that procedure is a straightforward potential resolution that frequently resolves the issue permanently.

When the Action Center shortcut is not available, rest assured that there are a few workarounds available. Even though this advice is for Windows 10, users of the new operating system might benefit from it as well.

What can I do if the Action Center in Windows 11 does not open?

Scanning the system files

1. In Windows 11, click the magnifying glass taskbar icon to bring up the search tool.
2. Within the search tool's text, type the keyword cmd.

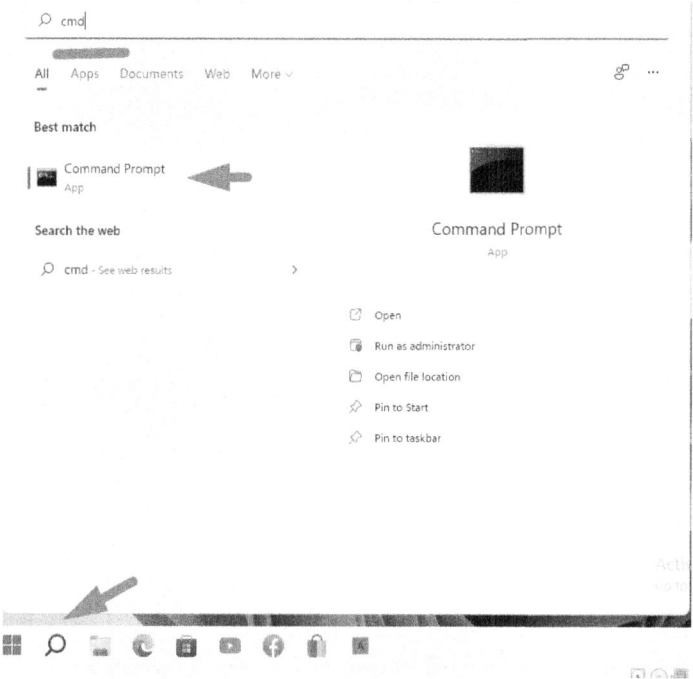

3. For the Command Prompt search result, click the Run as administrator option.

4. Enter the following DISM.exe /Online /Cleanup-image /Restorehealth scan command:DISM.exe /Online /Cleanup-image /Restorehealth

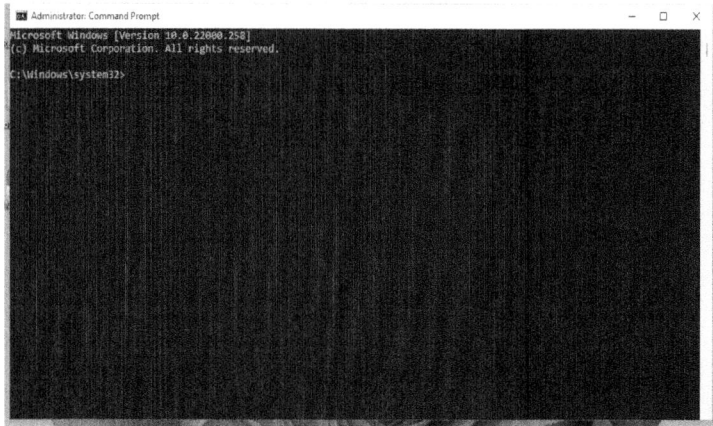

5. Once the first scan is complete, type the following command in the Prompt's window and hit Return: sfc /scannow

6. Wait until the system file scan reaches 100% completion. When the scan is complete, it will reveal the results.

Start File Explorer again

1. To begin, open the Windows 11 search box.

2. In the text field of the search tool, type the keyword Task Manager.

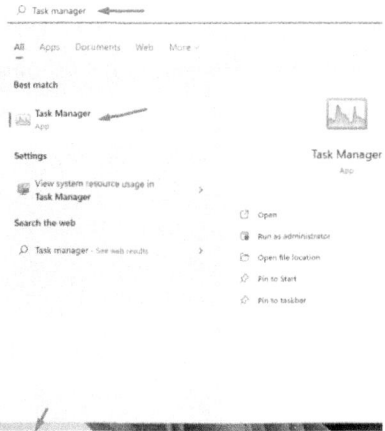

3. To open the Task Manager, click on it.

4. To begin, click the Processes tab.

5. Locate and pick Windows Explorer from the Windows Processes list.

6. Then click the Windows Explorer Restart button.

Using the Group Policy Editor, enable the Action Center

1. Select the Run shortcut from the menu by right-clicking the Start taskbar icon.

2. In the Open text box beneath the Run window, type the following command:gpedit.msc.

3. On the Run window, click the OK button.

4. Then, on the left side of the Group Policy Editor, click User Configuration, followed by Administrative Templates.

5. On the left side of the Group Policy Editor, click Start menu and Taskbar.

6. Then double-click the policy setting Remove Notifications and Action Center.

7. Select Disabled from the drop-down menu.

8. To apply the modified settings, click Apply.

9. Then, click OK to close the popup titled Remove Notifications and Action Center.

10. Finally, restart Windows once Group Policy Editor has been closed.

NOTE

Group Policy Editor is featured in Windows 11 Pro and Enterprise editions, but not in Windows 11 Home. However, in the Home edition, you can enable Group Policy Editor.

Renew the Action Center's registration

1. To access the search function, press the Windows key + S hotkey combination.

2. Then, in the search box, type PowerShell to locate that command-line utility.

3. To open Windows PowerShell, double-click it.

4. In the PowerShell window, type the following command:

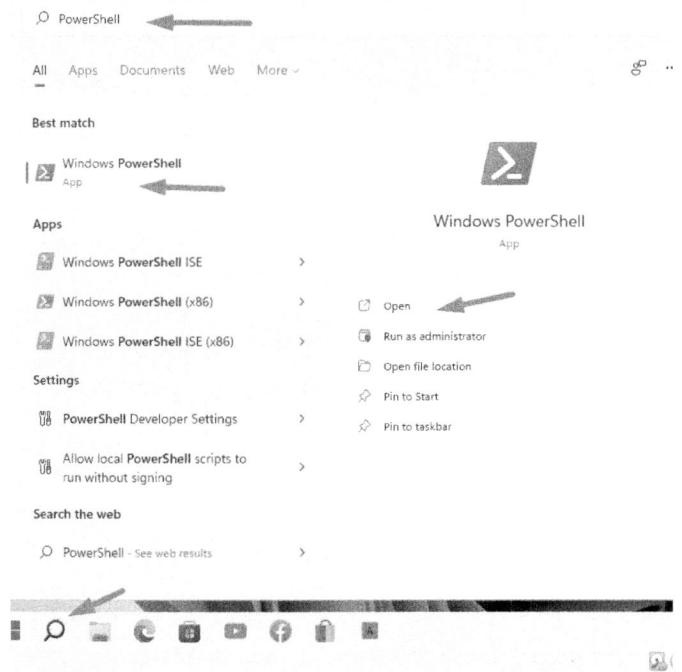

5. Add-AppxPackage   -DisableDevelopmentMode   -Register "$($_.InstallLocation)AppxManifest.xml"   -verbose   Get-AppxPackage | percent

6. To re-register the Action Center, press the Enter key.

7. After reregistering the Action Center, navigate to the Start menu. To restart Windows, click the Power and Restart choices there.

8. By modifying the register, enable the Action Center.

9. Bring up the search utility in Windows 11.

10. Type regedit in the search box to locate the Registry Editor.

11. To open the Registry Editor, click the search result.

12. Then you must open the following registry key:

13. Computer\HKEY_CURRENT_USER\Software\Policies\Microsoft\Windows

14. Within the Windows key, look for and select an Explorer key. If you are unable to locate it, right-click the Windows key in the left pane and choose the New and Key options from the resulting menu.

15. Then, you'll need to enter Explorer to determine the title of the new key.

16. To access the context menu for the Explorer key you just added, right-click it. Choose New and DWORD (32-bit).

17. Enter DisableNotificationCenter as the title of the new DWORD.

18. Now, double-click the DisableNotificationCenter DWORD to bring up a text box with the value data.

19. Assure that the new DWORD has the value 0 and click OK to close the window.

20. After that, restart your computer.

21. Restore a prior version of Windows 11

NOTE

Rolling back Windows 11 will erase all software installed after the date of your selected restore point. To determine which software will need to be reinstalled in order to create a restore point, under the System Restore box, select Scan for impacted programs.

Select the shortcut for Run by pressing the Windows key + X simultaneously.

1. To start System Restore, type the following text into the text box and click OK:
2. rstrui
3. If available, select the Choose a different restoration point option.
4. Continue to the list of restore points by clicking Next.
5. Select the Show more restore points checkbox if it is available.
6. Then select a restoration point that will revert Windows 11 to a time when the Action Center was accessible. If you're unsure, use the most distant date.
7. To proceed to the confirmation phase, click the Next button.
8. Select Finish to initiate system recovery for the specified date.

How has Windows 11's Action Center changed?

Microsoft has divided the Action Center in Windows 11 into two sections. It now comprises two distinct Quick Settings and Notification panels that may be accessed (typically) from the system tray.

The Action Center in Windows 10 consisted of a single panel that contained both settings and notifications. However, the Action Center is identical on both platforms, and with Windows 11, you have the option of customizing the Action Center.

It's unsurprising that Windows 11 users complain about the Notification panel not opening or the Action Center not launching at all.

If none of the above-mentioned probable answers resolves these issues, a last alternative is to reset Windows 11. This will reset the platform's factory default settings.

However, this is a last resort method because it requires reinstalling all software that did not come pre-installed on your PC. The process of resetting the platform is very similar to that of reinstalling it. Avoid it unless absolutely necessary.

What is a Notification Center?

Everything you need to know about notification management on a Windows 11 computer.

Microsoft's new Windows 11 operating system provides users with new desktop experiences and a more Mac-like user interface. It redesigned the entire operating system, from the user interface to the settings to the overall performance. Additionally, Windows 11 offers a redesigned Start menu, Taskbar, action center, and notification center.

Additionally, the notification center has been updated with softened sides and pastel hues. It has been moved from the Action Center hub above Quick Settings to the date and time system tray icon in the lower right corner of the display.

Notifications keep you informed of all activity on your system, informing you of critical emails, answers, missed Teams calls, and Windows updates, among other things. All of these notifications are grouped together in the Notification Center on Windows 11 devices. While notifications can be really useful, they can sometimes be rather unpleasant, interfering with your typical routine. As a result, it's occasionally preferable to disable notifications with Windows 11.

Windows 11 includes numerous options for customizing notifications to aid with productivity. We'll cover everything you need to know about managing notifications in Windows 11 in this article, including how to enable/disable notification for all apps or specific apps, disable alert messages, turn off notification sound, set notification priority, use focus assist, enable/disable notification banners, and turn off suggested notifications.

How to View Windows 11 Notifications

Whether a new email from a colleague arrives, a new device is discovered, a meeting reminder is sent, or software updates are installed, you receive notifications that inform you of what's occurring on your Windows 11 PC.

On Windows 11, alerts are displayed in the bottom right corner of the screen. By default, the notification banner will be displayed for 5 seconds before disappearing into the Notification Center.

Additionally, you may view the notification count near the Date and Time icon. The count indicates the number of notifications received from the specified apps or services. If you receive several notifications from the same application or service, the count will remain '1'. For example, if you get many emails to your default mail app, the count will display only one notice as a '1'. If you receive notifications from two distinct apps, the count will be two.

The notification center can be accessed by selecting the 'Date/Time' icon in the taskbar's right-most area or by hitting the shortcut key Windows+N. The compressed calendar will be positioned above the grouped notifications.

While the majority of notification banners are dismissed automatically to the Notice Center after 5 seconds, some alerts require you to accept/open or close the notification in order to dismiss it.

Notifications that have been dismissed will remain available in the Notification center. They will remain unresolved unless you manually remove them or open the notification.

You can open a notice by clicking on it. To dismiss the notifications, either click on the close button 'X' to close individual notifications or on the 'Empty all' button to clear the Notification center entirely.

Disable/Enable All Notifications in Windows 11

Notifications keep you aware of recent changes and developments, but the constant flood of notifications can become overwhelming and obnoxious at times. Thus, it is sometimes preferable to disable all notifications on your Windows 11 computer in order to avoid distractions. If you want to totally disable notifications from all apps and services, take these steps:

- To begin, open the Windows 11 Settings program by clicking the 'Start' icon and then selecting 'Settings', pressing Windows+I, or right-clicking the 'Start' button and then selecting 'Settings' from the overflow menu.

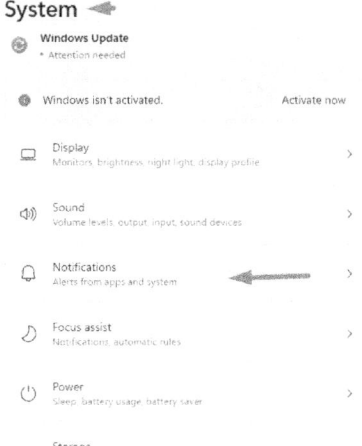

- Select the 'System' tab in the left sidebar of the Settings app and then the 'Notifications' option on the right.
- Turn OFF the toggle switch next to 'Notifications' on the following Notifications settings page. Simply click on the toggle to toggle between 'On' and 'Off'.
- You will no longer receive any notice on your machine at this time. To re-enable notifications on your PC, flick the switch next to 'Notifications' ON.

Disable/Enable Notifications from Specific Applications in Windows 11

By completely disabling notifications, you may miss some critical system notifications such as Windows updates, event reminders, and so on. At times, you may wish to enable/disable notifications for specific applications on your Windows 11 PC. In the majority of cases, manufacturer apps, social media apps, and other apps such as browsers can continuously pump out advertisements and spam messages. Disabling notifications from certain specific apps can assist you in concentrating on your task. This may be accomplished in two simple ways: through the Notification Center or through Settings.

Using the Notification Center to Manage Notifications for Specific Apps

In the Notification center, you may quickly disable notifications from a specific app. However, this method will only work if you already have a notification from the app for which you wish to disable notifications.

To open the Notification Center in Windows 11, click the Time/Date icon in the taskbar corner or press Windows+N. Navigate to a notification banner sent by an app for which you wish to disable notifications and select the 'horizontal three-dots' button. Select 'Turn off all notifications for *name of the app*' from the list of options. You will no longer receive notifications from that app.

Using Windows Settings to Manage Notifications for Specific Apps

Using the Settings app, you may disable/enable notifications for any particular app. To do so, click the Start button or press Windows+I to bring up Windows 11 Settings. Following that, select the 'System' tab and then the 'Notifications' option.

Once inside the Notifications settings page, scroll down to the 'Notifications from applications and other senders' area and choose the apps for which you want to disable notifications.

Using this section, you can activate or disable notifications for certain apps and senders. Once you've located the app for which you wish to disable notifications, change the toggle next to the app's listing to the Off position.

This will prevent all alerts from the disabled apps in the future. If you decide later that you want notifications from certain programs, you can always reactivate them by repeating the previous steps and activating the respective toggles.

Suggested Notifications on Windows 11: Disable/Enable

Microsoft frequently sends Windows tips and suggested notifications to promote various Microsoft goods and Windows features while you use the operating system. They frequently manifest as standard desktop notifications, which can be rather obnoxious and annoying.

For instance, you may get a notification advising you to configure capabilities such as OneDrive and backups, or recommending that you subscribe to Office 365 or Xbox Game Pass, among other things.

To disable suggested notifications on Windows 11, start by hitting Win+I to access Windows Settings. On the left pane, click the 'System' tab and then on the right, click 'Notifications.'

Scroll all the way to the bottom of the Notifications page to find two checks labeled "Offer advice on how to configure my device" and "Get tips and suggestions while I use Windows." Remove them both and you're finished.

There will be no more suggested notifications, and Windows will no longer tell you what to do with your PC. If you require assistance configuring your device or would like to get tips and suggestions from Windows, you can always enable the suggested notification by checking the boxes next to the appropriate options.

Windows 11: Enable/Disable Lock-Screen Notifications

By default, Windows 11 displays the contents of notifications on the lock screen. However, there are situations when this results in some privacy exposure, as the content of a social media app or message notification displayed on your lock screen can be viewed by others. Therefore, if you want a clean look on your locked screen, you can disable notifications via settings.

As seen in the preceding steps, open Settings and navigate to System > Notifications. On the Notifications settings page, click the drop-down menu labeled Notification (not the toggle).

This will provide several alternatives beneath the 'Notification' option. Remove the check mark next to 'Show notifications on the lock screen'. This will turn off all lock screen notifications.

Re-checking the option next to 'Show notifications on the lock screen' will re-enable the lock screen notifications.

Disable Notifications on the Lock Screen for a Specific App/Apps

You can also hide notifications from specific apps (such as Messenger, Skype, or Mail) from the lock screen.

On the Notification settings page, under the 'Notifications from applications and other senders' section, you may view a list of apps that have been granted permission to display notifications on the lock screen. Simply pick the app/apps from which you do not wish to view lock screen notifications.

For instance, if you want to conceal the 'Messages' app's alerts on the lock screen, simply click on the 'Messages' app (not the toggle).

Now, toggle the 'Hide content while notifications are on the lock screen' option to the off position.

To re-enable lock-screen notifications, set the 'Hide content while notifications are displayed on the lock screen' option to On.

Prioritize Notifications on Windows 11

When you're working on something essential, you probably don't want to be distracted by every unimportant notification, unless it's an emergency. For instance, you may wish to avoid missing any work-related alerts or updates from your favorite social media apps in the midst of the onslaught of notifications. In that instance, you can give select programs or services priority to ensure that you receive all notifications from those programs.

Navigate to System > Notifications in Settings. Select an app to prioritize in notifications under the 'Notifications from app and other senders' section.

Once the app's notification page is opened, you can change the priority of notifications by selecting one of the options 'Top', 'High', or 'Normal'. Set the priority to 'High' if you don't want to miss any app updates.

These priorities also dictate the order in which notification banners appear in the action center.

Prioritizing Notifications from the Notification Center

Additionally, you may customize the Notification Center's priority for your preferred or most critical apps to display alerts.

To begin, click the Notifications/Date and Time button in the taskbar to bring up the Notification center. Select a notification from a sender or app that you want to prioritize. Following that, click on the associated 'Settings' icon (three-dots menu).

Then, from the list of alternatives, select "Make app name> a high priority."

Mute Notifications Using the Focus Assist Feature

When you need to maintain concentration in order to complete critical tasks, when you're giving a presentation, or when you're utilizing a second monitor or projector to duplicate your display, you may wish to avoid interruptions at all costs. Then, you can temporarily mute notifications using the 'Focus Assist' feature.

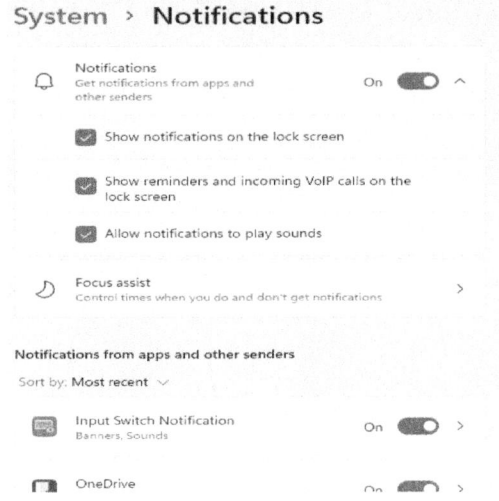

Focus Assist is a useful feature that was introduced in Windows 10 and has been retained in Windows 11. It enables you to reduce or entirely disable notifications when you need to maintain concentration for an extended length of time. When enabled, it disables notifications, audio, and alarms, allowing you to maintain focus.

While the Focus Assist feature is activated automatically in certain circumstances, you can also enable it manually or regulate the circumstances in which notifications are silenced. In a nutshell, this is Windows' 'Do Not Disturb' mode.

From the Action Center, toggle Focus Assist on/off.

By default, the Focus Assist is configured to activate automatically when certain conditions are met, such as when you're playing a game, duplicating your screen, or using a full-screen application. However, you can toggle 'Focus Assist' whenever you want.

System › **Focus assist**

Focus assist

To stay focused, choose which notifications you'd like to see and hear—the rest will go straight to notification centre where you can see them any time. **More about focus assist**

○ Off
   Get all notifications from your apps and contacts

○ Priority only
   See only selected notifications from the priority list
   Customise priority list

○ Alarms only
   Hide all notifications, except for alarms

☐ Show a summary of what I missed when focus
   assist was on

Automatic rules

⊙ During these times   Off ⬤   >
   11:00 PM - 7:00 AM: Priority only

To begin, click the set of three icons (Network, Sound, and Battery) in the taskbar's right-hand corner next to the clock and date, or press Windows+A to access the Action Center.

To activate 'Priority only' alerts, click/toggle the moon icon once. These alerts display only selected notifications from the priority list of apps. In Settings, you may change the priority list of apps.

Click/Toggle twice more to enable 'Alarms only' alerts. This option disables all notifications except for those associated with Alarms.

To completely disable the Focus help, click/toggle the icon once more.

From the Settings menu, toggle Focus Assist on/off.

Additionally, you can activate concentration mode in the Notifications Settings. Additionally, on the Focus assist settings page, you can choose which notifications are permitted and when they are permitted.

To begin, navigate to Settings > System > Notifications. Then, in the Notification settings, click on the 'Focus assist' option.

On the Focus assist settings page, you may pick between different focus modes and configure the focus aid. To manually enable focus assist, select a focus mode such as 'Priority only' or 'Alarms only'.

You can define which apps are permitted to send nonfiction when you select the 'Priority only' level. To choose which apps are prioritized, click the 'Customize priority list' option to the right of the Priority Only radio button.

You may manage which alerts are accepted and which are discarded directly to the Notification Center in the Priority list settings. By default, calls, text messages, and reminders are notified even when Priority attention mode is enabled; however, you can disable them if desired. To disable calls, text messages, and reminders, uncheck the boxes under the 'Calls, text messages, and reminders' section.

Additionally, you can add contacts to get notifications while concentrate mode is activated.

You may edit the priority list of apps in the Apps section. To add apps to receive notifications from, click the 'Add an app' icon. A pop-up window titled 'Choose an app' will display with a list of apps that you may add to the priority list. To add an app to the list, click on it.

To uninstall an app from which you no longer wish to get notifications, click on it and then on the 'Remove' button.

When you choose 'Alarm only' mode in the Focus assist, all notifications are disabled save for Alarms.

Additionally, you can control whether Focus Assist mode is triggered automatically by utilizing the choices in the 'Automatic rules' area. You can enable or disable the toggles according to your preferences.

Allow/Disallow Notifications for a Specific Time Period

If you want to control or suppress notice for a specified time period, you can specify the time period in the Automatic rules section.

Click on the 'During these times' option in the Automatic rules section of the Focus aids Settings page.

··· > During these hours

Choose when you want Focus assist to turn on.

On

Start time

| 11 | 00 | PM |

End time

| 7 | 00 | AM |

Repeats

Daily ∨

Focus level

Priority only ∨

☐ Show a notification in action centre when Focus assist is turned on automatically.

On the During these hours settings page, toggle the setting to 'On' and then use the drop-down menus to select the 'Start time' and 'End time' for the automatic focus assist.

Then, select 'Daily', 'Weekends', or 'Weekdays' from the 'Repeats' drop-down to repeat the automated trigger.

Additionally, the 'Focus level' drop-down menu allows you to select the focus mode (Alarms only or Priority only).

Activate/Deactivate Notifications While Playing a Game

You can toggle the 'When I'm playing a game' option under the

Automatic rules section to enable or disable notifications while playing the game. To adjust the level of concentration on this option, click on it rather than flicking the toggle.

Then, select either 'Priority only' or 'Alarms only' from the 'Focus level' drop-down menu.

Activate/Deactivate Notification Banners in Windows 11

Notification banners are little messages that appear along the lower right corner of your screen when anything occurs on your system (for example, when you receive a notification from an app). They come in a variety of shapes and sizes and display an overview of the notifications, although they often vanish after five seconds. Additionally, you may access the notifications through the Notification Center even after they have vanished from your screen.

Occasionally, you don't want to fully disable notifications; rather, you want to avoid seeing their banners on your screen while performing an important task. You may wish for the notifications to be automatically dismissed to the Notification center without appearing on your screen, so that you can review them later after your job is completed.

If you want to receive notifications but not the frequent notification banners that appear on your screen, then follow the steps below to eliminate the banners in Windows 11. Regrettably, there is no global setting in Windows 11 for deactivating notification banners for all programs; this must be done separately for each app.

To begin, navigate to the Notification Settings page in Settings by selecting System > Notifications.

Click on the app for which you'd like to disable banners under the 'Notifications from applications and other senders' section.

Then deselect the checkbox labeled 'Show notification banners'. Additionally, you may disable notifications for individual apps in the notification center by unchecking the 'Show notifications in notification center' option on the same settings page.

On Windows 11, you may customize the duration of notifications.

On Windows 11, notifications are typically displayed for no more than five seconds. Within five seconds of clicking/reacting to a notification, you will be taken to the app or service that delivered the message. If you do not click the notification, it will be transferred to the Notifications Center and will remain there until you act on it or dismiss it.

To begin, launch the Windows Settings application. Select the 'Accessibility' tab on the left sidebar of the Settings app and then the 'Visual effects' option on the right.

On the Visual effects page, you'll notice a drop-down menu labeled 'Dismiss alerts after this length of time'. By default, it's set to '5 seconds'.

To adjust the duration of when alerts are displayed, click on that drop-down and select a time period.

Activate/Deactivate Notification Sounds in Windows 11

Often, we are unaware of the alerts banners that appear in the corner of our screen, but it is the continual alert sound that annoys us and interrupts our work. In certain instances, you can disable notifications using the Notification settings.

Open the Notification Settings page and click the drop-down menu labeled 'Notifications.' Then deselect the button labeled 'Allow notifications to play sounds.'

You will no longer hear any notification sounds.

If you want to disable notification sounds for a single app or sender, navigate to the 'Notifications from applications and other senders' area and click on the app for which you want to disable notification sounds.

Then toggle the toggle next to 'Play a sound when a notice arrives' to the Off position.

Additionally, you can temporarily disable notifications using the Focus assist feature while still filtering alarms and other high-priority items.

Show/Hide Notification Badges on Windows 11 Taskbar Icons

Badges are the small counters on an app's icon that indicate when something new has been added to the app. Notification badges can be displayed on taskbar app icons such as the You Phone or Mail icons to indicate the amount of notifications or new SMS/email messages in the related app.

To begin, open Windows Settings, click 'Personalization' in the left-sidebar, and then on the right, click 'Taskbar' settings.

Click the 'Taskbar Behaviors' drop-down on the Taskbar settings page.

Personalisation > Taskbar

Taskbar corner icons
Show or hide icons that appear on the corner of your taskbar

Pen menu
Show pen menu icon   Off
when pen is in use

Touch keyboard
Always show touch   Off
keyboard icon

Virtual touchpad
Always show virtual   Off
touchpad icon

Taskbar corner overflow
Choose which icons may appear in the taskbar corner – all others will
appear in the taskbar corner overflow menu

Taskbar behaviours
Taskbar alignment, badging, automatically hide, and multiple displays

Get help
Give feedback

It will display a list of available options. To display or hide the badges (unread message counter) on taskbar apps, check or uncheck the box next to the 'Show badges (unread message counter) on taskbar apps' option.

Now, anytime you receive a new message or notification in the taskbar messaging or social networking app, you'll see a badge with a counter directly above its icon indicating the number of unread messages or alerts in the app.

Bonus: 10 Tips to know before installation

On October 5, Windows 11 will begin rolling out to eligible computers. If you intend to update, there are various steps you should take before manually initiating the process, including verifying hardware compatibility, setting appropriate security features, and creating a backup of the present setup.

Verify that your computer is capable of running Windows 11

While Windows 11 is a free upgrade for existing Windows 10 machines, this does not guarantee compatibility with your device. The new operating system has increased the minimum system requirements, which means that one of the first things you should do before continuing with the installation is to verify that your computer's hardware fits the criteria.

Follow these procedures to determine whether a PC is compatible with Windows 11:

1. Access the download page for PC Health Check.

2. Click the Download PC Health Check app button under the "Check for compatibility" section.

3. Double-click the WindowsPCHealthCheckSetup.msi file to initiate the installation.

4. Accept the terms of the License Agreement by clicking the I accept the conditions of the License Agreement option.

5. Install by clicking the Install button.

6. Open Windows PC Health Check is a checkbox option.

7. To conclude, click the Finish button.

8. Click the Check now option under the "Introducing Windows 11" section.

9. (Optional) Select the See all results option to see a list of components that passed the compatibility check.

10. (Optional) Click the button for device specs.

Once you've completed the procedures, you'll receive a notification indicating that you can upgrade to the new version if your hardware is compatible. If the hardware is incompatible, you will receive an error notice explaining why the device is not capable of running version 21H2.

TPM 2.0 must be enabled in the BIOS.

To improve security, Windows 11 requires the Trusted Platform Module (TPM) version 2.0 chip. If the device lacks this capability, you will be unable to do an in-place upgrade or a clean installation.

To ensure that TPM 2.0 meets the Windows 11 requirements, follow these steps:

- Navigate to Settings.
- Update & Security can be accessed by clicking on it.
- Select Recovery.
- Click the Restart now option under the "Advanced startup" section.
- Select Troubleshoot.
- Select the Advanced tab.
- To access the UEFI Firmware settings, choose the UEFI Firmware settings option.
- Restart the program by clicking the Restart button.
- Depending on the motherboard, select the advanced, security, or boot settings page.
- Select the TPM 2.0 option and enable it.

If your computer lacks a TPM 2.0 chip and you have an AMD CPU, the module is most likely integrated into the processor, and the choice will be labeled "fTPM" (firmware-based TPM 2.0) or "AMD fTPM switch." If the device is powered by an Intel processor, the security feature is referred to as Platform Trust Technology (PTT).

If the device does not include a TPM option and this is a custom build, you may be able to add support via a module. Ensure, however, that you examine the motherboard manufacturer's website to confirm that support is available.

Following these procedures, the Windows 11 check should pass, allowing you to upgrade the PC to the new operating system.

Secure Boot should be enabled in the BIOS

Secure Boot is an additional security feature that is necessary for Windows 11 installation. This is a module that ensures the computer boots using only the software recommended by the manufacturer.

If your device is still running on the legacy BIOS (Basic Input Output System), you must first convert the MBR (Master Boot Record) drive to a GPT (GUID Partition Table) format and then switch to UEFI (Unified Extensible Firmware Interface) mode and activate Secure Boot. Otherwise, the machine will not boot if you enable the newest firmware. If you're performing a clean installation, you can skip this step; however, if you're upgrading from the Windows 10 desktop, this is required.

Use the following procedures to enable Secure Boot prior to installing Windows 11 (version 21H2):

- Navigate to Settings.
- Update & Security can be accessed by clicking on it.
- Select Recovery.
- Click the Restart now option under the "Advanced startup" section.
- Select Troubleshoot.
- Select the Advanced tab.
- To access the UEFI Firmware settings, choose the UEFI Firmware settings option.
- Restart the program by clicking the Restart button.
- Depending on the motherboard, select the advanced, security, or boot settings page.
- Select "Secure Boot" and then "Enabled."

Almost all machines with UEFI firmware feature Secure Boot, but if yours does not, you'll need to upgrade your system or consider purchasing a new computer that fulfills the Windows 11 criteria.

Following these steps, the computer should pass the hardware certification procedure, allowing you to continue with the in-place upgrade or clean install of Windows 11.

Create a complete backup of your PC.

A backup is possibly the best recovery technique if something goes wrong during or after the installation. While you can use any third-party backup program, Windows 10 still has a built-in system image backup.

To build a complete backup of your computer, connect a USB storage device with sufficient space and follow the steps below.

1. Navigate to the Control Panel.
2. Select System and Security from the menu.
3. Select Backup and Restore.
4. From the left pane, select the Create a system image option.
5. Choose the option "On a hard disk."
6. Choose an external hard disk to use as a backup for your device.
7. Continue by clicking the Next button.
8. To begin the backup process, click the Start backup button.

Once all of the procedures are completed, the backup process will begin. You will be prompted to build a recovery disk, but you can skip this option because you can access the recovery settings using a Windows 10 installation USB media.

Along with a comprehensive backup, it's a good idea to backup your files to an external storage device or cloud storage service such as OneDrive. Additionally, you can use this instruction to set up your computer's automatic file backups.

Remove incompatible and non-essential applications

During the process of upgrading to a new version of Windows, poorly designed software or third-party security solutions such as antivirus can cause issues that prevent you from completing the Windows 11 installation. As a general rule, uninstall incompatible applications prior to updating to avoid issues.

Follow these procedures to uninstall programs on Windows 10:

- Navigate to Settings.
- Select Apps.
- Select Applications & features.
- Select the app from the "Apps & features" section (or game).
- Quick tip: If you have a large number of apps, you can use the search box, "Sort by," and "Filter by" choices to locate an app more quickly.
- Uninstall the program by clicking the Uninstall button.
- Again, click the Uninstall button.

- A quick note: If you're deleting a classic desktop application, follow the on-screen instructions to complete the process.

Once these procedures are completed, the program will be deleted from the device. You may need to repeat these steps to uninstall any other programs that are incompatible with the Windows 11 21H2 installation.

Spare on your computer

While Windows 11 requires a hard disk with a minimum of 64GB of available space, the device will still require approximately 20GB of available space to complete the installation.

You can use these procedures to identify which files consume the most space and to determine what items you may need to delete to free up some space.

Following these procedures will help you free up space on Windows 10:

- Navigate to Settings.
- Select System.
- Select Storage.

- Select the Temporary files option under the "Local Disk (C:)" column.

- Examine the temporary files you wish to eliminate in order to clear up space.

- Select the Delete files option.

System › **Storage**

Local Disk (C:) - 49.3 GB

19.8 GB used   29.5 GB free

Apps & features   3.80 GB/19.8 GB used ›

Temporary files   500 MB/19.8 GB used ›

Show more categories

Storage management

Storage Sense
Automatically free up space,
delete temporary files, and   Off ›
manage locally available cloud
content

Cleanup recommendations
Looking for items to clean   ›

Following these procedures, Windows 10 will clear up the drive, freeing up space for the Windows 11 installation.

Apart from temporary and other files, programs and games can use up a lot of space. If this is the case, follow the previous steps to free up space on your computer by uninstalling apps and games.

Verify and correct system errors

If you've been using the same installation for an extended period of time, the setup is likely to have corrupted files and other issues that will prevent the upgrade from succeeding. If you're performing an in-place upgrade, you may use the Deployment Image Servicing and Management (DISM) and System File Checker (SFC) command-line tools to identify and resolve any issues that may prevent Windows 11 from installing correctly.

- Start the program.
- Conduct a search for Command Prompt, right-click the first result, and choose Run as administrator.
- To fix the Windows image, use the following command and press Enter:
- DISM /Online /RestoreHealth /Cleanup-Image
- To correct the installation, type the following command and press Enter:
  /scannow SFC

Once these procedures are completed, the SFC utility will repair the system files using the locally corrected image files created by the DISM tool. The log files will be stored in the percent windir percent /Logs/CBS/CBS.log and percent windir percent /Logs/DISM/DISM.log directories, which you can read to obtain additional information about the procedure.

Disconnect all peripherals that are not absolutely necessary

When you plan to update to a new version of Windows, there is a possibility that hardware conflicts will prevent the installation from succeeding.

For instance, storage devices (such as USB flash drives and external hard drives), printers, and cameras attached to the computer during the installation process can create errors and other issues. As a result, it is recommended that you disconnect any peripherals prior to installing version 21H2.

Bluetooth can also create complications. Disable any devices that use this wireless technology prior to updating by going to Settings > Devices > Bluetooth & other devices and turning off the Bluetooth toggle switch.

All you need is a monitor, keyboard, and mouse, as well as an internet connection. After the installation is complete, the devices can be reconnected.

Along with these instructions, you'll want to ensure that you begin the Windows 11 upgrade process with an administrator account. Additionally, if you're performing an in-place update, it's a good idea to take note of your installed apps and custom settings to ensure that you can rearrange the system appropriately if any of these items are lost during the process.

Customer reviews

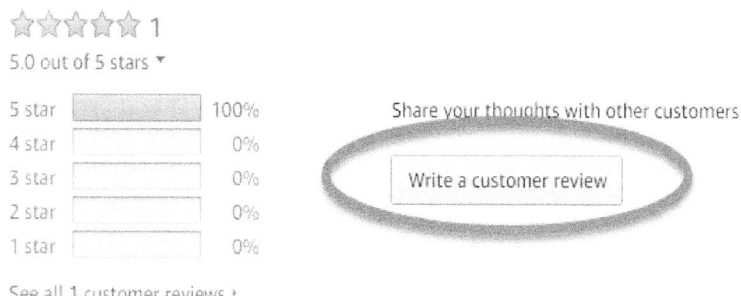

☆☆☆☆☆ 1

5.0 out of 5 stars ▾

5 star		100%
4 star		0%
3 star		0%
2 star		0%
1 star		0%

Share your thoughts with other customers

Write a customer review

See all 1 customer reviews ›

I would be incredibly thankful if you could take just 60 seconds to write a brief review on Amazon, even if it's just a few sentences!

>>Click here to leave a review

Conclusion

While Windows 11 looks significantly different from Windows 10, the two operating systems are fairly similar on the inside. With the new operating system now available on some devices — and via Microsoft-mandated upgrades — comparing Windows 11 to Windows 10 has never been more critical.

The two are quite dissimilar visually. However, there are significant internal changes that distinguish the next version of Windows from the current iteration. You're undoubtedly wondering whether you should upgrade, and we've got you covered with this comparison of the two.

Should you upgrade from Windows 11 to Windows 10?

As with Windows 10, which was a free upgrade for users of Windows 8.1 and 7, Windows 11 will be a free upgrade for users of Windows 10. However, there is a catch. That upgrade is only valid if your PC meets Microsoft's minimal criteria — which have already sparked some debate, particularly with relation to the TPM 2.0 requirement.

If you own a Surface device or a new device from one of Microsoft's partners, you will automatically receive Windows 11 when it becomes available on October 5. New devices that are still running Windows 10 will be able to upgrade via Windows Update. Following that, Microsoft says it would use a staged approach, with upgrades expected to reach all compatible PCs by the middle of 2022.

However, there is another option: the Installation Assistant enables you to install Windows 11 on a suitable PC as soon as it becomes available. Although Microsoft does not encourage this route, it is likely that some hardware will create problems, and you may encounter a few bugs or Blue Screens of Death.

If your device is compatible, you should consider upgrading to Windows 11 and giving it a try. However, there is a catch. After upgrading, you'll have only ten days to revert to Windows 10. Microsoft will maintain Windows 10 until 2025, but after that 10-day downgrade window, you'll need to perform a clean install (erasing all your data).

There are a few things to be aware of if you plan to upgrade. Windows 11 deprecates some features introduced in Windows 10.

You may no longer sync your desktop background, Internet Explorer and the Math Input panel have been deleted, and some applications have been eliminated as well. Three-dimensional viewer, OneNote for Windows 10, Paint 3D, and Skype are among the apps included. However, those are still available at the store. If you're concerned,

Microsoft maintains an exhaustive list.

If you're a gamer, take note that Windows 11 includes some features that are tailored specifically for you. Auto HDR enhances the vibrancy of your games, while Direct Storage enables speedier communication between your graphics card and SSD.

Performance of Windows 11 vs. Windows 10

When compared to Windows 10, Windows 11 does have the ability to improve your computer's performance. In a YouTube video, Microsoft discussed the performance gains and optimizations included in Windows 11. In general, the performance improvements in Windows 11 are largely due to the way the newer OS manages system tasks, which are typically visible when you open Task Manager.

According to Microsoft, Windows 11 performs extensive memory management in order to prioritize the application windows that are open and operating in the forefront. This should ensure that they have priority over other system resources when it comes to CPU power. Microsoft demonstrated this by demonstrating how, even at 90% CPU load, the Excel program in Windows 11 launches quickly, despite the CPU being overworked. The company asserts that the same is true for Windows 11's "shell," which drives the Start Menu and other visual elements.

Other efficiency improvements in Windows 11 affect how your computer wakes up from sleep and manages standby time. In comparison to Windows 10, Microsoft stated that Windows 11 allows RAM to remain powered while the PC is in sleep mode, ensuring that it retains power while the rest of the system does not. This will assist your PC in waking up up to 25% faster from sleep.

Additionally, because the Edge browser is the default browser in Windows 11, you should observe significant performance gains as compared to using the browser on Windows 10. According to Microsoft, the sleeping tabs function can help you save 32% on memory and 37% on CPU consumption.

The final set of efficiency enhancements pertains to disk footprints and browser caches. Microsoft enhanced its usage of compression technology in Windows 11. In non-critical applications such as Sticky Notes, the default rate is a "stub." This means that while the program is loading, binaries from the system are fetched on-demand without impairing the app's functionality. This can assist lower the size of an app's disk footprint and reduce background update and download activity. Microsoft claims that the browser cache now consumes less disk space.

Bugs in Windows 10 vs. Windows 11

Microsoft's latest operating system is Windows 11, whereas Windows 10 has been available for five years. With that in mind, you can anticipate Windows 11 to have a slew of other bugs and flaws that may damage your system's performance.

True, Windows 10 is also not a bug-free operating system. Although it has experienced device-breaking faults in the past, Windows 11 is currently experiencing a fair share of concerns that you may want to examine before upgrading.

The most serious flaw in Windows 11 affects AMD CPUs. This is the point at which AMD CPUs may reduce or restrict performance by up to 15% in games. However, AMD and Microsoft have since published a remedy.

Another issue with Windows 11 is memory leaks. As we confirmed and tested, Windows 11 may consume additional RAM when numerous instances of the File Explorer are opened. It never releases RAM when the File Explorer is closed, and the system consumes additional resources. This is not a widespread issue, and it has also existed in Windows 10 for some time, but it is significant to say the least.

Another flaw could result in empty folders being created in critical subsystem locations, even if the folders have no effect on performance or use up much space. These folders end in.tmp, which indicates that Windows is deleting the contents of the folders but not the folders themselves. A minor issue in comparison to the ones we've discussed.

The final big problem affects File Explorer once again. Certain customers have reported that the context menu in Windows 11 opens slowly. This is the context-sensitive menu that appears when you right-click an item. Again, this is not an issue that affects everyone. Microsoft said that it is aware of the issue and that a remedy has been included in a Windows Insider build.

We've only touched on a couple, but Windows 11 includes an excellent tool for tracking issues. Windows users can always use the Feedback Hub to report new bugs. If you sort by new or top, you'll see all the minor Windows 11 defects that are too many to include in a single post. Therefore, if you're truly interested in what's going on there, search for Windows 11 feedback in the app on your Windows 10 PC.

Menu Start Taskbar

When comparing Windows 11 to Windows 10, the most noticeable differences are the Start Menu and the Taskbar. Microsoft has centered the Taskbar and Start Menu on the screen in Windows 11. This gives it a more MacOS and ChromeOS-like appearance. You may, however, reposition it to the left if desired.

In terms of the Start Menu, it has been simplified in Windows 11. You only see a static list of applications, followed by a list of your most frequently used documents. You can expand your applications, go through the list, and pin applications as desired. While this may sound familiar, it is critical to remember that Windows 11 discontinues support for Live Tiles. If you're serious about seeing information in your Start Menu at a glance, Windows 10 is the finest option.

With regards to the Taskbar, it's worth noting that Windows 11 introduces some significant modifications in comparison to Windows 10. Microsoft has reduced the size of the search box to an icon and deleted Cortana functionality in Windows 11. To use Cortana, you must first download the program. Additionally, search has been relocated to the center of the screen, with a floating style and tabbed layout reminiscent of Windows 10.

Even the Windows Timeline has vanished. Windows 11 deprecates that Windows 10 capability in favor of the sync capabilities of Microsoft Edge. Virtual Desktops have taken the place of Windows Timeline.

However, if you wish to pin your Taskbar to the right or left side of the screen, we have some bad news for you. This is no longer possible, as the Taskbar in Windows 11 is fixed to the bottom. Additionally, apps cannot alter the taskbar.

Many of these modifications are purely cosmetic. Windows 11 and Windows 10 both have the same features; the visual appearance is what differs.

Multitasking and support for external monitors

You may have seen Microsoft's multitasking demonstration in Windows 11 and wondered if it will make the jump to Windows 10. As far as we are aware, this is a Windows 11-only feature that will not be included in Windows 10.

Snap Layouts in Windows 11 enable you to improve multitasking and system performance by grouping your windows and saving them to the taskbar. When you hover your cursor over the maximize button, you can tile windows of varying sizes. This will not be available in Windows 10. It retains the classic "Snap" functionality, which requires manually tiling your windows using a keyboard combination or by hovering to a specific side of the screen.

There is also a notice on external displays. Windows 11 remembers how you configured your windows on your external display and saves them in that configuration when you unplug and reconnect a monitor. This is one of the most vexing issues with Windows 10, which Windows 11 resolves.

Tablet-like mode

Windows 10 includes a classic tablet mode, which transforms your PC into a full-screen Start Menu environment. This is no longer necessary in Windows 11.

Rather than that, Windows 11 operates more like an iPad, where switching to a tablet makes things easier to touch. When you touch your window with your finger, you'll notice an effect. Additionally, Microsoft included motions for opening and closing windows, navigating between desktops, and expanding the Windows Ink Workspace's capabilities. All of these are not in Windows 10's tablet mode, which many found confusing.

Microsoft Store

In the future, the app store in Windows 11 and Windows 10 will be very similar, but with one significant distinction. The app shop in Windows 11 now supports Android apps via the Amazon Appstore, however it is currently only available in the Windows Insider beta channel. That is not available in Windows 10 due to Windows 11's reliance on the new Windows Subsystem for Android.

The newly rebuilt Microsoft Store in Windows 11, which simplifies the process of finding apps and movies, will soon make its way to Windows 10, albeit without Android apps. The shop continues to offer access to all Windows applications across both operating systems. This comprises Win32 applications, Universal Windows Platform applications, and Progressive Web Applications.

This is part of a bigger push by Microsoft to increase the number of programs available in the Microsoft Store. The business revealed that the Epic Games Store will be available through the Microsoft Store and that Microsoft will not take a percentage of revenues. Microsoft has stated in statements that this is to make the Microsoft Store a one-stop shop for all of your PC applications.

As previously stated, Windows 10 will also receive an improved Microsoft Store. The main difference is that Windows 11 now supports Android apps, which was not available at launch. We do not yet know when they will arrive.

Compatibility

For many, the distinction between Windows 10 and Windows 11 is purely cosmetic. Windows 11 introduces the first significant change to the supported CPUs since Windows 8.1 was released. To run the most recent version of the OS, you'll need an Intel Core 8th-generation processor or above, or an AMD Ryzen 2000 processor or higher.

This effectively eliminates support for a large number of PCs. Intel's eighth-generation processors arrived in late 2017, while AMD's Ryzen 2000 processors appeared in 2018. In short, if your machine is more than four years old, it is likely that Windows 11 will not support it. That may be the decisive point in favor of it over Windows 10.

Additionally, TPM 2.0 — which is included on the great majority of current PCs — and UEFI Secure Boot are required. If your processor is supported, you should not have to worry about these two additional needs. For years, Microsoft has mandated certain characteristics from its manufacturing partners.

There is a way to install Windows 11 on hardware that is not supported, but we do not encourage it. Although Microsoft has not confirmed it, the corporation has made a strong implication that unsupported users will be excluded from vital security updates. If you wish to continue installing, you may do so via the Media Creation Tool, which bypasses hardware checks.

Cycle of support and updates

Windows 11 abandons Windows 10's semi-annual upgrade cycle in favor of a single annual update. That is identical to MacOS. Microsoft has pledged to support Windows 10 until 2025, during which time it should continue to get updates.

We're unsure whether it will continue to receive twice-yearly feature upgrades, but if you're looking for the latest and greatest version of Windows, Windows 11 is the place to be. Additionally, if you want the most secure version of Windows, you may wish to update to Windows 11. Microsoft has made numerous statements about how safe Windows 11 is as a result of TPM 2.0 requirements and Secure Boot.

Printed in Great Britain
by Amazon

84586243R00098